A brilliant reference with a focus on introdu
challenges. The danger with AI and software tes
understand it all. This book addresses this issu                    ...o a rich
source of references and useful concepts using t              ...nd references, to
both stimulate and challenge the reader's own kn                ...his broad subject. Highly
recommended.

**Paul Mowat** *MBCS CITP, BCS SIGiST, Social Media Secretary & Committee*
*Member & Quality Test Engineer Director, Deloitte UK*

AI-based systems conquer more and more areas of our daily life. People are concerned whether these systems are trustworthy. *Artificial Intelligence and Software Testing* tackles this issue and provides an insight into AI quality and how it differs from conventional software quality, and where the difficulties and challenges are in testing machine learning systems. A great introduction into this topic and must read for all interested in building AI-based systems that you can trust.

**Klaudia Dussa-Zieger**, *Chair GTB & Vice President ISTQB®,*
*Head of ISTQB® Certified Tester AI Testing (CT-AI) Taskforce*

In the ever expansive and evolving virtual domain, the prominence of AI is becoming more and more prolific, and this evolution will not be without its challenges. This title provides an excellent resource into the potential dilemmas faced in this evolutionary field as the virtual, cognitive, and physical spaces become more interlinked with the dawn of the metaverse. The part that humans play in the growth, development and testing of AI is discussed. Supported by a wealth of experience, research, and evidence from the authors, the title provides a great introduction to and understanding of AI and software testing. Highly recommended for all with an interest in this area.

**Jonathan Miles** *MBA BSc(Hons) FCMI, Head of Strategic Intelligence, Mimecast*

Shift Right! A concept you won't find in 'The Seven Principles of Testing'. *Artificial Intelligence and Software Testing* puts the principles into perspective. Not only does it explore early testing, but it also looks at the concept of exhaustive testing thoroughly and effectively. As a trainer of software testing I will definitely use all this book has to offer. Guiding the next generation of testers to question the intricacies of machine learning. A must for anyone in tech, not just software testers.

**Rachel Hurley** *MBCS TAP.dip, Technical Trainer (Software Testing)*

As the title describes, this book is a robust AI and ML testing exploration that also dives into the juxtaposition of the trustworthiness and bias in AI systems. It touches on the basis of ontologies and how to enable the considerable impact of testing and monitoring of AI-based systems. After reading this you would be able to answer an important challenge: how to determine that your AI system has been extensively tested.

**Dina Dede**, *AI/ML and Cloud Architect Lead, UK*

This book beautifully captures the game-changing complexity of artificial intelligence (AI) and the traditional discipline of software quality management. It is a comprehensive manual addressing the conundrum and tantalizing promise of both disciplines with good pace and a distinct future-present context. Forget waterfall and DevOps, we're right shifting into OpsDev, AIOps and digital twins in the metaverse, so things are about to get a whole lot more interesting. Excellent effort, and a much-needed treatment of this topic by true experts.

**Jude Umeh** FBCS CITP, Senior Program Architect, Salesforce

*Artificial Intelligence and Software Testing* is a great read. The vast experience of the authors is evident as they comprehensively explain the challenges and benefits of not only applying AI to testing, but also testing the AI software itself. I found the insight into the shift-right approach and its application during the development of the test and trace application fascinating. A must read for any testing/QA professional plus any C-suite looking to rapidly increase their ROI on testing.

**Anil Pande**, Managing Partner, TestPro Consulting Ltd

This book is a very good introduction to using AI in software testing as well as testing AI systems, covering several relevant topics like societal risk, bias, ethical behavior, quality, trustworthiness, and the problems associated with AI/ML systems. I specifically liked the section that details the problems associated with AI/ML systems. I would recommend this book to anyone who is starting their study on software testing vis-a-vis AI/ML systems.

**Venkat Ramakrishnan**, Software Quality Leader and Software Testing Technologist

*Artificial Intelligence and Software Testing* is a valuable resource for anyone curious in how to approach testing AI models as they expand into our daily lives. This is a clear, informative read which discusses within each chapter different testing challenges with AI software and advice on how to handle them effectively. I can highly recommend this to testers and students alike.

**Katy Hannath** BSc(Hons), MSc in Artificial Intelligence and
Data Science Student, & Quality Assurance Tester, VISR Dynamics

This book is an exceptionally practical resource which is a remarkable reference guide to understanding the foundations of AI and ML for anyone wishing to build a career in AI or define a test approach. It has a clear, direct, and concise explanation of AI, ML, ethics, ontology, quality, bias, challenges, test automation, and the significance of 'shift-right' testing. It offers thorough, data-driven and real-world examples that bring together the rich wealth of experience from these expert authors and authorities in this area.

**Boby Jose** BSc MBA MBCS, Author of BCS publication
Test Automation: A manager's guide

What an exciting and relevant publication! Beyond the positive game-changing societal benefits delivered by AI, it has proven equally disruptive to all aspects of software engineering including software testing. This book provides great insight into new build and test design techniques to augment our traditional thinking. An essential guide for technology leaders and test professionals alike, looking to understand how to approach the critical problem of building and testing today's complex and often unpredictable AI systems.

**Jack Mortassagne**, *Director at Cigniti Technologies and TMMI Accredited Assessor*

This is a great book for those who want to gain more insight into how AI will affect the software testing profession. The writers introduce the challenges in AI in an easy-to-understand manner, while the case studies showcased are extremely interesting and contemporary, clearly exemplifying the topics presented. Brilliant read and highly recommended!

**Dr Diana Hintea** *BEng(Hons) PhD SFHEA, Associate Head of School (School of Computing, Electronics and Mathematics), Coventry University*

In a time the promised paradigm shift of artificial intelligence is starting to have a real-world impact, this is a vitally important book. It explains the social, ethical, and technical concerns around AI in an easy to understand way, making a complex subject easily accessible. Everyone involved in IT is likely to be impacted by AI whether from a business, technical, ethical, or quality point of view and so this book will be an invaluable resource for everyone in IT. As a Testing and Quality specialist, this is going to have pride of place on my bookshelf as a practical, real-world reference for helping me navigate testing and quality in the emerging world of AI.

**Bryan Jones** *MBCS, Director of Testing Practice, Sopra Steria Private Sector*

This book is a must-read for anyone in software testing with responsibility for quality assuring AI technology that must engender public trust. With topics that feel both familiar and challenging, the authors confidently explore a range of subjects to broaden and deepen the reader's understanding of the intersection of AI and testing.

**Bronia Anderson-Kelly**, *IT Change Consultant, Sabiduria Ltd*

# ARTIFICIAL INTELLIGENCE AND SOFTWARE TESTING

## BCS, THE CHARTERED INSTITUTE FOR IT

BCS, The Chartered Institute for IT, is committed to making IT good for society. We use the power of our network to bring about positive, tangible change. We champion the global IT profession and the interests of individuals, engaged in that profession, for the benefit of all.

### Exchanging IT expertise and knowledge
The Institute fosters links between experts from industry, academia and business to promote new thinking, education and knowledge sharing.

### Supporting practitioners
Through continuing professional development and a series of respected IT qualifications, the Institute seeks to promote professional practice tuned to the demands of business. It provides practical support and information services to its members and volunteer communities around the world.

### Setting standards and frameworks
The Institute collaborates with government, industry and relevant bodies to establish good working practices, codes of conduct, skills frameworks and common standards. It also offers a range of consultancy services to employers to help them adopt best practice.

### Become a member
Over 70,000 people including students, teachers, professionals and practitioners enjoy the benefits of BCS membership. These include access to an international community, invitations to a roster of local and national events, career development tools and a quarterly thought-leadership magazine. Visit www.bcs.org/membership to find out more.

### Further information
BCS, The Chartered Institute for IT,
3 Newbridge Square,
Swindon, SN1 1BY, United Kingdom.
T +44 (0) 1793 417 417
(Monday to Friday, 09:00 to 17:00 UK time)
**www.bcs.org/contact**
**http://shop.bcs.org/**

# ARTIFICIAL INTELLIGENCE AND SOFTWARE TESTING
## Building systems you can trust

Adam Leon Smith, Rex Black, James Harold Davenport, Jeremias Rößler, Joanna Isabelle Olszewska and Jonathon Wright

Edited by Adam Leon Smith

bcs
The Chartered Institute for IT

Permission to reproduce extracts from British Standards is granted by BSI. British Standards can be obtained in PDF or hard copy formats from the BSI online shop: www.bsigroup.com/Shop or by contacting BSI Customer Services for hardcopies only: Tel: +44 (0)20 8996 9001, Email: cservices@bsigroup.com.

Published by BCS Learning and Development Ltd, a wholly owned subsidiary of BCS, The Chartered Institute for IT, 3 Newbridge Square, Swindon, SN1 1BY, UK.
www.bcs.org

Paperback ISBN: 978-1-78017-5768
PDF ISBN: 978-1-78017-5775
ePUB ISBN: 978-1-78017-5782

British Cataloguing in Publication Data.
A CIP catalogue record for this book is available at the British Library.

Disclaimer:
The views expressed in this book are of the authors and do not necessarily reflect the views of the Institute or BCS Learning and Development Ltd except where explicitly stated as such. Although every care has been taken by the authors and BCS Learning and Development Ltd in the preparation of the publication, no warranty is given by the authors or BCS Learning and Development Ltd as publisher as to the accuracy or completeness of the information contained within it and neither the authors nor BCS Learning and Development Ltd shall be responsible or liable for any loss or damage whatsoever arising by virtue of such information or any instructions or advice contained within this publication or by any of the aforementioned.

All URLs were correct at the time of publication.

**Publisher's acknowledgements**
Reviewers: Andrew Lowe
Publisher: Ian Borthwick
Commissioning editor: Rebecca Youé
Production manager: Florence Leroy
Project manager: Sunrise Setting Ltd
Copy-editor: Gillian Bourn
Proofreader: Barbara Eastman
Indexer: Matthew Gale
Cover design: Alex Wright
Cover image: Istock/oonal
Typeset by Lapiz Digital Services, Chennai, India
Printed by Hobbs the Printers Ltd, Totton, Hampshire, UK

# CONTENTS

# LIST OF FIGURES AND TABLES

# ABOUT THE AUTHORS

## ADAM LEON SMITH

Adam Leon Smith FBCS is Chief Technology Officer of Dragonfly, a European consultancy, training and products firm that specialises in the intersection of AI and quality. Adam also runs regular training courses in testing, test automation and testing issues related to AI systems. In addition, he is the current Chair of BCS Special Interest Group in Software Testing (SIGiST), the biggest non-profit testing group in the UK. Adam has held senior roles at multinational financial services institutions, as well as ambitious start-ups; he is focused on applying verification and validation techniques to complex systems and emerging technologies. He is very active in ISO/IEC's Artificial Intelligence standardisation community, where he leads the ISO/IEC projects on AI bias, and a standard for extending systems quality models to cover AI. Adam is a Fellow of BCS, and a Director of ForHumanity, an independent oversight body auditing the use of emerging technology. He is a regular speaker at conferences and a resident podcaster for the Ministry of Testing and Fuzzy Quality, a podcast dedicated to quality, testing and AI. You can contact Adam on twitter (@adamleonsmith) and by email: adam@disc0tech.com.

## REX BLACK

With 40 years of software and systems engineering experience, Rex Black is President of RBCS (www.rbcs-us.com), a software and systems engineering and testing leader, providing consulting, training and expert services. Since its founding in 1994, RBCS has served over 1,000 clients on six continents, spanning all areas of software and system development, from embedded systems to gaming software to banking and insurance to defence systems to pharmaceuticals and health care. Rex has worked with clients from small start-ups to Fortune 20 global enterprises. He has experience helping clients apply software and systems engineering and testing best practices in a wide variety of development life cycles, including Kanban, Scrum, DevOps, Waterfall and Spiral. Rex has provided expert services as part of a software quality oversight organisation under the Office of Inspector General and as an expert witness on multiple lawsuits, including one $180 million breach of contract case. He is also the most prolific author practising in the field of software testing today, having written 14 books and dozens of articles over the last 20 years. He is Founder and past President of the ISTQB and of the ASTQB and Founder and President of TMMi America. You can contact Rex on twitter (@RBCS) and by email: rex_black@rbcs-us.com, via LinkedIn: www.linkedin.com/in/rex-black, or via his website: www.rbcs-us.com.

## DR JAMES HAROLD DAVENPORT

James Davenport TD MMath MA PhD DSc (Hon.) FIMA CMath FBCS CITP NTF. After studying at the University of Cambridge, working at IBM Research and teaching in Cambridge and Grenoble, James Davenport joined the University of Bath in 1983, first as a lecturer, then professor, Head of School, Director of Information Technology, High Performance Computing Champion and most recently as a Theme Lead for the Institute of Coding. He has also taught in Cambridge, Sweden, China, Italy and at numerous French universities and Grandes Écoles, and held research sabbaticals at GMD in Germany, at Western University and University of Waterloo (Canada), and New York University, as well as IBM Research and Microsoft Research. His main research interests are in computer algebra and cryptography/security. However, both subjects are very concerned with counter-examples and worst cases, rather than just reflecting the optimism of many software developers, so the mindset translates naturally to looking at AI ethics, or rather the potential lack thereof. As a former Vice-President (Academy) of BCS, and a long-time professional accreditor, he has long been concerned about the role of legal, social, ethical and professional issues in computing education. He believes that AI has changed the details, but not the principles. James can be contacted on: masjhd@bath.ac.uk.

## DR JOANNA ISABELLE OLSZEWSKA

Dr Joanna Isabelle Olszewska BSc(Hons) MSc(EPFL) PhD(UCL) CEng CSci FBCS FHEA SMIEEE is a British computer scientist. She is a lecturer (Assistant Professor) with UWS, UK, and leads research in Algorithms and Softwares for Intelligent Vision Systems. A Senior Member of IEEE, she stands on the IEEE Artificial Intelligence Standard Committee, and she is part of the IEEE Global Initiative for Ethical Considerations in Artificial Intelligence and Autonomous Systems. She has been invited to be panel speaker at the University of Edinburgh Union on 'The Future of AI'. She has given talks, including at ENS Paris, at conferences such as ICRA, at symposiums such as ACM Sacramento FWS, and at events, such as the Canadian Mathematical Society (CMS) Anniversary Meeting, as well as interviews, including for the BBC Lunch Time 'Women in Engineering' Program. She has been TPC member of over 100 international conferences such as IJCAI and has chaired over 70 conference/workshop sessions, such as at IROS. She has contributed to 11 ISO/IEC/IEEE standards in various roles, including Vice-Chair of ISO/IEC/IEEE P41062, and she has authored 100+ peer-reviewed publications and three book chapters. She holds several awards, including, ESWA Outstanding Reviewer Award, and distinctions, including ACM Distinguished Speaker, and she has been supervisor for 60 BSc(Hons)/MSc/PhD students, including the supervision of the Best BSc Thesis awarded by the GCHQ Prize and the supervision of the Best MSc Dissertation awarded by the AGD Prize. Joanna can be contacted by email on joanna.olszewska@ieee.org.

## DR JEREMIAS RÖßLER

Dr Jeremias Rößler has a PhD in Computer Science from Saarland University and more than 10 years of experience as a software developer and tester. He is the founder and CEO of @retest_en (https://retest.de), a German-based start-up that brought AI to test automation. Today he is working at SAP. His refreshingly unusual approach to test automation (difference testing, patents pending in US and Europe) has many advantages over conventional test automation and he shows how to combine it with AI to overcome the oracle problem. Difference testing is open source for web (https://github.com/retest/recheck-web) and enables 'unbreakable' and autohealing tests. He is one of the authors of the A4Q 'AI and Software Testing' certification syllabus. He has been a speaker at many international conferences, both in academia and industry. Attendees call his talks visionary and amusing. He is a writer, blogger (https://dev.to/roesslerj/), developer and computer scientist. He is married, has two children and lives in Germany. If you ever meet him in person, he is very approachable and enjoys to be talked to, so don't be shy. You can contact him easily on Twitter (@roesslerj) or LinkedIn (https://www.linkedin.com/in/roesslerj/).

## JONATHON WRIGHT

Jonathon Wright is a strategic thought leader and distinguished technology evangelist. He specialises in emerging technologies, innovation and automation, and has been an international commercial experienced practitioner within global organisations for more than 20 years. He is currently the Chief Technology Evangelist for Keysight Technologies based in Silicon Valley. Jonathon combines his extensive experience and leadership with insights into real-world adoption of Cognitive Engineering (Enterprise AI and AIOps). Thus, he is frequently in demand as a speaker at international conferences such as TEDx, Gartner, IDC, Oracle, AI Summit, ITWeb, EuroSTAR, STAREast, STARWest, UKSTAR, Guild Conferences, Swiss Testing Days, Unicom, DevOps Summit, TestExpo and Vivit Community (of which he is currently the president of the largest independent software community with over 80,000 members across 125 countries). During the coronavirus pandemic he was the Quality Engineering lead for MIT for the COVID Paths Check foundation. He is also a member of Harvard Business Council, AI Alliance for the European Commission and involved with the review committee for the ISO-IEC 29119 part 8 'Model-Based Testing' and part 11 for the 'Testing of A.I. based systems' as a committee member in BCS SIGiST. Jonathon also hosts the QAlead.com podcast (based in Canada) and is the author of several award-winning books (2010–2021) and online courses. Jonathon can be contacted on: jonathon.wright@keysight.com.

# ABBREVIATIONS

| | |
|---|---|
| **ACM** | Association for Computing Machinery |
| **AI** | artificial intelligence |
| **AI-T** | artificial intelligence-based system testing ontology |
| **ANN** | artificial neural network |
| **API** | application programming interface |
| **APM** | application performance management |
| **AR/MR** | augmented and mixed reality |
| **BDD** | behaviour-driven development |
| **BLO** | Basic Linux Ontology |
| **BoK** | body of knowledge |
| **CI/CD** | continuous integration/continuous deployment |
| **CORA** | core ontology for robotics and automation |
| **CQ** | competency question |
| **CRS** | cloud robotics systems |
| **CSV** | comma separated values |
| **DL** | description logic |
| **DOLCE** | descriptive ontology for linguistic and cognitive engineering |
| **DX** | digital experiences |
| **EDA** | exploratory data analysis |
| **EO** | enterprise ontology |
| **ETL** | extract, transform and load |
| **EU** | European Union |
| **GAEN** | Google Apple Exposure Notifications |
| **GDPR** | General Data Protection Regulation |
| **GPS** | global positioning system |
| **GPX** | GPS exchange format |
| **GUI** | graphical user interface |
| **HAL** | hardware abstraction layer |
| **HIPAA** | Health Insurance Portability and Accountability Act |
| **HRPA** | human resource participation |
| **I4.0** | Industry 4.0 |

| | |
|---|---|
| **IA** | intelligent agent |
| **IEC** | International Electrotechnical Commission |
| **IEEE** | Institute of Electrical and Electronics Engineers |
| **IoT** | Internet of Things |
| **ISO** | International Organization for Standardization |
| **ISTQB** | International Software Testing Qualifications Board |
| **IT** | information technology |
| **ITOM** | IT operations management |
| **IVS** | intelligent vision system |
| **KR** | knowledge representation |
| **LTP** | Linux Test Project |
| **MAS** | multi-agent system |
| **MBT** | model-based testing |
| **ML** | machine learning |
| **MSE** | mean square error |
| **NFT** | non-fungible token |
| **NIST** | National Institute of Science and Technology (US) |
| **NLP** | natural language processing |
| **ODE** | ontology-based software development environment |
| **OSOnto** | operating system ontology |
| **OWL** | Web Ontology Language |
| **PAE** | process and activity execution |
| **PRPA** | procedure participation |
| **RDF** | Resource Description Framework |
| **ROCO** | cloud-robotic-system domain ontology |
| **ROI** | return on investment |
| **ROoST** | Reference Ontology on Software Testing |
| **RPA** | resource participation |
| **SDLC** | software development life cycle |
| **SoS** | System of Systems |
| **SQL** | Structured Query Language |
| **SRT** | site reliability testing |
| **STOWS** | Software Testing Ontology for Web Service |
| **STVO** | spatio-temporal, visual domain ontology |
| **SUMO** | suggested upper merged ontology |
| **SWEBOK** | Software Engineering Body of Knowledge |
| **SwTO$^I$** | Software Test Ontology Integrated |
| **TaaS** | Testing-as-a-Service |
| **TOVE** | Toronto virtual enterprise |

| | |
|---|---|
| **UFO** | unified foundational ontology |
| **UI** | user interface |
| **UK** | United Kingdom |
| **UML** | Unified Modeling Language |
| **US** | United States |
| **UX** | user experiences |
| **W3C** | World Wide Web Consortium |
| **WPPA** | work product participation |
| **WWW** | World Wide Web |
| **XAI** | explainable artificial intelligence |
| **XML** | Extensible Markup Language |

# GLOSSARY

**Acceptance testing:** Test level that focuses on determining whether to accept the system.*

**Adversarial attacks:** Where an attacker slightly perturbs (changes) the inputs to a model in order to influence its prediction(s).

**AIOps:** Industry category for machine learning analytics technology that enhances IT operations analytical capabilities.

**Automated reasoning:** Advanced area of computer science that is concerned with applying reasoning in the form of logic to computing systems to make inferences automatically.

**Automation bias:** Cognitive bias that occurs when a human decision-maker favours the recommendations of an automated decision-making system, over other inputs.

**Black-box test technique:** Test technique based on an analysis of the specification of a component or system.*

**Chaos engineering:** Discipline of experimenting on a software system in production in order to build confidence in the system's capability to withstand turbulent and unexpected conditions.

**Classification:** Machine learning (ML) function that predicts the output class for a given input.

**Component testing:** Test level that focuses on individual hardware or software components.*

**Concept drift:** Change in users' expected predictions from a model that is presented with the same input data.

**Data pipeline:** Infrastructure supporting an ML algorithm. It includes acquiring data, pre-processing and preparation, training one or more models and exporting the models to production.

**Digital twin:** The generation or collection of digital data representing a physical object.

**Hyper-parameter:** Variable set by a human in an ML model, before training the model.

**Integration testing:** Test level that focuses on interactions between components or systems.

**Knowledge representation:** Study of how to put knowledge into a form that a computer can reason with.

**Neural network:** Network of two or more layers of neurons, connected by weighted links with adjustable weights, which takes input data and produces an output. Also called an artificial neural network.

**Neuron:** Node in a neural network that takes input values and produces an output value, by combining the input values and applying an activation function to the result.

**Ontology:** Explicit specification of a conceptualisation.

**Reasoning:** Form of AI that generates conclusions from available information using logical techniques.

**Regression:** ML function that outputs continuous (typically, floating point) values.

**Reinforcement learning:** Task of training a model that makes decisions to maximise an objective, using a process of trial and error.

**Shift left:** Shifting the focus of testing effort towards the early design and testing phase, that is, shifting to the left of the systems or software development cycle.

**Shift right:** Shifting the focus of testing effort towards testing with users in a production environment.

**Sub-symbolic AI:** System based on techniques and models, using a numeric representation and implicit information encoding.

**Symbolic AI system:** System based on techniques and models, using symbols and structures.

**System testing:** Test level that focuses on verifying that a system as a whole meets specified requirements.*

**Test coverage:** Degree to which specified coverage items have been determined or have been exercised by a test suite expressed as a percentage.*

**Test level:** Specific instantiation of a test process.*

**Test oracle:** A source to determine an expected result to compare with the actual result of the system under test.*

**User acceptance testing:** Type of acceptance testing performed to determine if intended users accept the system.

**Validation:** Confirmation, through the provision of objective evidence, that the particular requirements for a specific intended use or application have been fulfilled.*

**Verification:** Confirmation, through the provision of objective evidence, that specified requirements have been fulfilled.*

**White-box test technique:** Test technique only based on the internal structure of a component or system.*

**XPath:** Query language for selecting nodes in XML.

*Copyright © International Software Testing Qualifications Board (hereinafter called ISTQB®).

# PREFACE

This book is a journey through a number of topics relating to AI and quality, which is a hot topic for practitioners, as well as policy-makers and academics.

AI quality is different from conventional software quality. Chapter 2 of this book explains why that is, covering topics from bias to drift. We talk about these issues from a quality perspective, but many of them are of keen interest to practitioners who would not normally consider themselves interested in quality. For example, those who are more focused on the ethical application of AI, or the legal issues surrounding AI, are likely to worry about bias and drift. In fact, the proposed European Union (EU) AI Act at the time of writing, is mostly focused on the management of technical quality management systems for AI.

One of the more complex issues is unintended bias, which can arise from different sources, and can have significant legal and societal effects. This is explained in detail in Chapter 3, from a conceptual as well as a mathematical perspective.

Chapter 4 moves on to the complexities and challenges in testing machine learning systems, which make up the largest proportion of AI deployments today. This chapter is particularly useful for practitioners planning to obtain the ISTQB Certified AI Tester qualification.

Then we will pivot in Chapter 5 to cover how AI can be used to support software testing processes. While this is almost the inverse of testing AI, many of the same issues – such as bias and drift – need to be considered.

Next, in Chapter 6, we explore the more advanced topic of ontologies. Ontologies are basically formal representations of knowledge that we have, in this case about testing. By establishing ontologies we can allow automated reasoning through AI to further support testing.

Finally, as the earlier chapters will have explained that AI is in need of constant monitoring for quality issues, we explore some examples of shift-right testing and AIOps in Chapter 7.

# 1 INTRODUCTION

## Rex Black

I've always loved the ocean. When I'm close to an ocean – provided it's not too cold or the weather too inclement – I like to swim or SCUBA dive in it. One of the things about oceans, though, is that oceans have waves and currents. Some are gentle, some a little more sizeable and some are massive. The massive ones can be dangerous if you don't know what you're doing, but serious surfers search these massive waves out and have the time of their lives in them. I've always envied those surfers, flying down the face of an enormous wave, though I've never learned to do it myself.

The software industry is like an ocean: there are always waves of change coming, of various sizes. The big ones can be exciting if you have the skills to catch them, but they can also swamp your career, as lots of software testing professionals who pooh-poohed the Agile wave have learned in a painful fashion.

Another big wave – which oddly enough has been decades in coming – is artificial intelligence (AI). I took a class in AI as a senior at UCLA, and worked on a proof-of-concept project for a professor to use AI in stock trading. This was in 1988. Slow wave, but now it's finally here, bringing real change to the real world.

So, in this book, you're going to read about the skills you need to ride this wave as a test professional. As a test professional already, you probably know that one key part of your job is to ask questions and understand risks. So, what are some of the questions, risks and skills that this book will raise and enhance?

One key question is whether we can trust AI, especially given some of the crucial roles it will play (e.g. self-driving cars). Any time you have objects moving in the physical world – beyond just electrons whirring around in silicon and circuitry – you have the possibility of damage, injury or death. Yes, software has long been involved in making potentially dangerous objects move in the real world – think avionics software or implantable medical devices – but AI promises to make encounters with software-driven moving objects a daily, if not hourly, experience for all but those who choose to live as hermits. As software testing professionals, how can we help ensure that society can trust these systems to be more beneficial than risky?

Of course, we would do that by testing the AI systems; but how can we test AI systems, especially since the most common form, machine learning, will change its behaviours in response to our tests? This is a marked difference from traditional software that, under most circumstances, will give the same output for the same inputs over and over again provided the software is not changed. This book gives some ideas on how to attack this challenge.

The point of running a test is, of course, to learn something, to get a result. We always prefer that result to be definitive, to be able to say the test passed or failed, not to say, 'Well, maybe that worked.' But what does 'passing a test' even mean for an AI? There may not be a clear specification of correct behaviour, or correct behaviour may change over time, or we may not even know what correct behaviour is beyond what the software tells us. At one time, the solution to this kind of problem was to create a parallel system, an approach that was once favoured for certain high-criticality systems, but is no longer in wide use. In this book, you'll read about some ways to approach this challenge as well.

This change in what we get in terms of test results means that test metrics will be different, too. For example, functional testing of traditional systems often involves looking at the percentage of tests that pass versus those that fail. For AI systems, the correct questions for functional tests are likely to be, 'How often does each test give a result that appears correct?' or 'How far from the expected result values are the results of each test?'

## THE CHALLENGES OF TESTING AI

To some extent, testing AI systems will be harder because the problem space is harder than many of us are used to dealing with as test professionals.

AI systems are being used to deal with complex, chaotic, messy realities, where the number of possibilities is huge, even compared to existing software, such as software that plays chess (which has somewhere on the order of $10^{123}$ moves) or Go (which has more than $10^{360}$ moves; see Koch, 2016). As both of these numbers are greater than the number of atoms in the universe, it's not like we are used to solving only trivial problems. However, in thinking about self-driving cars consider the number of possible driving routes from any location in the United Kingdom (UK) or Germany or the United States to any other location within the same country. Obviously, that's a much less constrained set of possibilities than moves on a chess board or a Go board, so the number of possible outcomes is much larger.

Not only are the problems harder, but AI systems are different. AI systems change in response to stimuli, unlike other software that only changes when updated deliberately. AI's change in behaviour is driven by the stimuli, not predetermined like other software updates. So, the testing itself will influence how the system will behave next.

Historically, we have used computers to automate activities that humans are bad at (doing the same thing the exact same way over and over again) or that take too long to do manually (complex maths or accounting). Now, we are trying to use computers to automate activities that have complexities that don't easily lend themselves to mathematical formulas but which humans learn to do as children.

People and data have biases, and these can become embedded in AI systems. For example, the relative number of women in IT is smaller than the number of men, which can lead an AI to be biased in favour of men when deciding who is more likely to succeed in an IT role. Broad-based use of AI systems resulting in the calcification and reinforcement of such biases is a significant societal risk that must be addressed, and test professionals must be aware of and responsive to managing that risk.

This risk is compounded by the fact that people trust computers too much. That may seem odd to you and me, because, as test professionals, we have learned to be very sceptical of software. We tend to expect it to fail. However, many people don't have that outlook, but rather assume, 'Well, if the computer says so, that must be right.'

Another challenge to the test professional arises because the world constantly changes, which means AI systems will change too. Consider the COVID-19 pandemic. When I first heard of a strange respiratory disease in China, I thought, 'Yeah, I bet this will be like SARS and MERS, something that will be contained and maybe a little freaky but not a huge deal.' Well, I was completely wrong about that. When testing AI systems, we'll need to think about not just small, incremental changes, but big, fast, disruptive changes like pandemics, otherwise we risk missing important tests.

Stepping back a bit to consider the objectives of testing, one typical objective is to reduce risks to the quality of the software to an acceptable level. However, traditional quality models don't adequately capture quality for AI systems. For example, traditional software either gives the correct answer for a given set of inputs or it doesn't. AI systems may give correct answers sometimes and not others for the same inputs, or may give an answer that is different from the expected but still correct, or may give different results for inputs that are in the same equivalence partitions and thus would (traditionally) be expected to be handled the same way. This means that we will need to re-think our testing techniques.

We will also need to re-think how we measure test coverage. Just based on what has been said so far, you've probably guessed that requirements, design and other specification coverage measurements clearly won't work, and that will be reinforced in a moment when I get to the probabilistic rather than deterministic behaviour of AI systems. Other common dimensions of coverage, such as risk coverage and supported configurations, may be relevant, but do they take the place of specification coverage? Further, since we aren't using traditional programming, code coverage – always of limited use for measuring completeness of testing in any case – is even less useful, if not utterly useless. This book will help you to understand how to approach this critical problem for testing AI systems.[1]

Because AI systems often change in response to inputs, it's important that such changes be desirable. For example, deliberate malice or simply exposure to the wrong data could result in an AI becoming racist, as happened on one occasion with a Twitter bot (Vincent, 2016). Of course, the very idea of an artificial intelligence becoming racist is surreal, almost Kafkaesque, on multiple levels. 'Not intelligent enough to pass a Turing test but capable of directing hateful comments at others who could pass a Turing test' is a statement that perhaps could describe more than just racist bots, but also some people one might have the misfortune to meet, but that's a question outside the scope of this book.

How do we test for ethical and unethical behaviour? In a situation where grey areas or known ethical conundrums exist, how to handle it? For example, a runaway street car could plough into a crowd of people where it may kill over a dozen, unless a person (or in this case an AI) acts on it to shunt it onto another track where it will only hit one person

---

1    For more on possible ways to think about test coverage, see my presentation 'Dimensions of Test Coverage' (Black, 2015).

but will certainly kill them. If that seems simple, consider a self-driving car where a dozen careless bicyclists recklessly swerve in front of it.[2] Should it avoid hitting them by turning onto a sidewalk where a single law-abiding pedestrian will be struck? What constitutes correct behaviour here? What constitutes ethical behaviour? How do we program such behaviour? How do we test for it?

Over recent years, regulators in the UK, EU and the United States (US) have struggled with issues of data privacy. However, when behaviour can vary from one set of inputs to another, how do we test for compliance with regulations, such as data privacy? For example, in the US, access to patient information is regulated under a law called Health Insurance Portability and Accountability Act (HIPAA). Testers must be able to test for compliance or non-compliance with such laws, but can we be confident that the results of our tests will not change as the AI evolves?

So, what is our role as quality professionals in social issues? Of course, as individuals, we may choose to donate to one cause or another, or participate in demonstrations for or against something or someone, but those are personal choices. With AI systems, we may find our work thrust into the middle of some very thorny matters. For example, the market for home ownership in the United States has some extremely fraught social history revolving around race.[3] If you have ever worked as a software tester, software engineer, business analyst or other software professional in banking, you may be aware of the regulations associated with ensuring the banks no longer perpetuate the damage that was done to racial minorities who were systematically disadvantaged in home loans in the United States. Outside that domain, your professional involvement in this area may have been limited. Now, with AI systems, as this book will explain, to the extent that the systems you are working on can influence social outcomes (for good or evil), you may find yourself professionally engaged in evaluating whether those systems are having malign effects, which may be both inadvertent and quite subtle.

As this book will further explain, to the extent that your work testing AI systems has an intersection with social issues, it will be complicated by various biases. 'I'm not biased', you might protest, and you might well be right, but are the data that were used to train your AI biased? Is your AI biased through some other means? In what way? How can you test to ascertain whether such biases exist?

In testing these AI systems, the hard-won test design techniques that we have accumulated over the years, especially in the work of pioneers like Glenford Myers and Boris Beizer, such as equivalence partitioning, boundary value analysis, decision tables, state diagrams and combinatorial testing, may lose some of their power, because of what Beizer referred to as the 'bug assumption' behind each technique.[4] The bug assumptions are the types of bugs each technique was particularly powerful at finding, and those types of bugs are the types of bugs that occur in traditional procedure and object-oriented programming. In AI systems, other types of bugs exist, and some of the bugs that we find in traditional programs are less likely. In this book, you'll gain insights into new test design techniques, to augment the traditional techniques, for testing AI systems.

---

2   This is discussed by Malcolm Gladwell (2021) in an episode of the podcast *Revisionist History*.

3   For one account of this history, see Richard Rothstein's *The Color of Law* (2017).

4   See Boris Beizer's book *Software Testing Techniques* (1990) for more on the bug assumptions behind each technique.

We are used to software working the same way (at least functionally) every time it is used to solve the problem with the same set of inputs. However, for non-functional behaviours like reliability and performance, we often see probabilistic behaviour, where reliability can be expressed in terms of percentage likelihood of the system failing under a given level of load or the percentage of responses that are received within a given time target under a given level of load. For AI systems, functional behaviours can also be probabilistic, in addition to evolving over time. This is another factor that makes it difficult to find reliable test oracles for functional testing of AI systems.

Of course, one of the bright shiny objects in testing has been, for decades, test automation. Tool vendors have made large amounts of money, often by deploying trendy buzzwords and promising easy success and quick return on investment (ROI), but my clients and I have found that test automation, in the long run, is less likely to succeed than open-heart surgery. Over 80 per cent of otherwise-healthy people 70 years or older who have open-heart surgery are still alive five years later (Khan et al., 2000), but less than half of major test automation efforts I've seen with my clients are still achieving a positive ROI, using the same strategy and technologies, after five years. In this book, you will learn how AI will affect test automation. Just as importantly, you'll learn how it won't affect test automation, and the obstacles that stand in the way of certain AI benefits for test automation in the short term, so that you are less likely to get snowed by a buzzy sales pitch from a tool vendor.

Automated tests can work at multiple levels and through various interfaces. The level of testing and the interface of automation change the challenges associated with applying AI systems to the test automation problem. However, the fundamental challenges associated with test automation at each level and through a particular interface often do not change just because an AI is being applied, though it is – of course – very much in the interests of the boosters of the test automation tools to assert the contrary. This book will help you to define the right criteria for test automation tool evaluation, which is critical in any test automation project. As always, a strong business case and demonstrable ROI is essential for any major endeavour, and test automation – whether done with AI or not – will almost always be a major endeavour. Remember, too, that return on investment must be measured against clearly defined objectives, and those must be the right objectives.

As should be clear by now, all these challenges and differences associated with testing AI systems have implications for skills. For example, suppose you are testing an AI system that helps make high-frequency stock trades. In addition to needing serious domain expertise in terms of financial systems, financial markets and financial regulations – all skills necessary for testing such systems implemented with traditional technologies – you may also need serious data science and mathematical skills, due to the probabilistic nature of the system.

These skills are necessary to deal not only with the more complicated test oracle problem associated with an AI-driven high-frequency trading system (which is a hard enough problem with a traditional implementation), but also with the thorny problem of test data design. In fact, test data design is complicated enough that, while test professionals should understand the process, it often must be done by a professional data scientist. The test professional's grasp of the test data design issues serves primarily for them to act as a reviewer for the work of the data scientists in this regard, to deal with various biases that could affect the validity of their work.

Just because testing of AI systems abounds with new challenges, new risks and new skill requirements, doesn't mean that the old risks and skills are obsolete. For example, when assembling a System of Systems – and, in this Internet-of-Things world, just about everything talks to everything else and thus just about everything is a system-of-systems – we must ensure that each component system has been properly tested in a manner reflective of the way in which they will be used. Testing of the data flows across the interfaces is a place where the traditional test design skills of equivalence partitioning, boundary value analysis and combinatorial testing will be necessary.

There are other things that won't change, too. It's long been established that the longer a defect exists, the more it will cost, both in terms of impact on the project, the system and its users and in terms of cost to remove. These costs are not primarily associated with the discrete act of changing a few lines of code – after all, once the defect is found in the code, the effort to change the code doesn't change that much – but rather with finding the defect to begin with, and mitigating the consequences associated with the failures the defect causes. To address this, smart software engineers for decades have talked about shift left, meaning finding and removing defects as close as possible to the point of introduction.

However, another way to reduce the time from introduction to discovery of defects can include shifting right. Shifting right has to do with making the discovery of defects that do escape into production as quick, painless and cheap as possible. How can AI systems help us do this? Read on to find out.

## SUMMARY

So, you are holding in your hand – or on your favourite electronic reading device – a book that will introduce you to a number of new ideas and new challenges related to testing and quality of AI systems. This book can start you on your journey, but it can't provide easy solutions to all the challenges, because challenges don't always have easy answers.

But, as I've noted above, there are places where the tried-and-true still apply. Beware the person who comes to you saying, 'This changes everything', and listen to their words with inherent scepticism. However, when we're talking about AI, it is hard to imagine a situation where AI doesn't prove highly disruptive to all aspects of software engineering, including software testing. After all, some inventions really do change everything, or at least change a lot of things. Many people on this planet would not be here if it weren't for a breakthrough by Fritz Haber, a man almost no one has heard of but whose idea touches about half the people in the world every day, every time they eat food.[5]

---

[5]  Fritz Haber invented a process used to create ammonia, which is essential to the manufacture of chemical fertilisers. Sadly, Haber also was central to the invention of chemical warfare, which makes his legacy of change mixed. Tragically, in spite of Haber's contributions to the German war effort in the First World War, members of his family died in concentration camps during the Second World War because of his Jewish heritage. A quick summary of Haber's complex life, career and contributions to science is found at: https://en.wikipedia.org/wiki/Fritz_Haber

By reading this book, you'll gain some insights into the AI-driven disruptions that are headed your way – if not already on top of you – and, if I may modify my metaphor mid-sentence, give you ideas about how to ride that wave of disruption rather than being swamped by it. I wish you success as a software test professional as you ride the wave into the world AI will change, possibly as much as Haber's invention did. Let's hope that, unlike Haber's invention, we don't end up using AI – artificial intelligence, non-human intelligence – to create new, more efficient ways of being inhumane to each other. Part of that is up to each of us.

# 2 AI TRUSTWORTHINESS AND QUALITY

**Adam Leon Smith**

Artificial intelligence (AI) has been around since the 1950s and has now become the new electricity and a 'must-have' for many businesses. The increasing uptake of AI is unlocking the technology's true potential and delivering efficiencies in many sectors, not just in the bleeding-edge applications we hear about in the press, but in more menial and everyday ways on devices in your home, on your phone and in the workplace.

AI is hard to define, the definition evolves as fast as the technology. The description that perhaps has the most consensus is applying acquired knowledge to make decisions, usually in contrast to using more explicit logic (conventional programming). This presents both new opportunities and new problems for software and systems quality specialists.

AI can help to automate quality and testing-related activities, but many engineers are struggling with the challenges involved in evaluating and describing the quality of AI systems, and managing the new risks associated with integrating AI components. One of the most difficult areas is the imperfection inherent in statistical systems, and difficulty in reproducing and explaining results. Another challenge is convincing everyone that AI systems can be trusted with important decisions. In this chapter we will explore these problems and discuss a model that can be used to define AI quality.

## TRUSTWORTHINESS

There are concerns from buyers, regulators and end-users of AI technologies about their 'trustworthiness' at the point of use. It is important to consider this at the point of use because these concerns are not in the research lab but increasingly part of the wider digital transformation of the public and private sector.

BCS conducted a survey (BCS, 2020a) that found that 53 per cent of UK adults have no faith in any organisation to use algorithms when making judgements about them. Similarly, in the US, a large-scale survey found that a majority of respondents expressed concern about specific use cases for algorithm use, including personal finance scores (Smith, 2018). A normalised and representative study across the 28 EU states also found that 74 per cent of respondents want more rigorous controls on the use of algorithms (Grzymek and Puntschuh, 2019).

The definition of trustworthiness seems to depend heavily on context, and might be simply the characteristics of systems that make people want to trust them.

So why do people use the term trustworthiness? Trust is very much a human quality; some people are undoubtedly thinking of systems taking near human form and being reliable and dependable like a human might be. Some are probably thinking more about the accuracy and bias issues exhibited in systems that have been shown to treat people differently based on attributes that make people uncomfortable. Some are probably just worried about the inherent statistical accuracy issues that are present when you use probability to infer logical conclusions.

The definitions of quality and trustworthiness are different but linked, and there are different definitions of trustworthiness. The EU High-Level Expert Group on AI defines trustworthy AI as 'lawful (respecting all applicable laws and regulations), ethical (respecting ethical principles and values) and robust (both from a technical and social perspective)' (High-Level Expert Group on Artificial Intelligence, 2020).

We can compare that definition to quality, which is defined by ISO/IEC as 'degree to which a set of inherent characteristics fulfils requirements' (ISO, 2005). One difference between these two linked definitions is that quality requires specification by stakeholders.

Considering the EU view, there is a requirement for systems to deliver against implied legal, ethical and social requirements as well as explicit ones. A second definition currently under development at the time of writing within the international standardisation community defines technology trustworthiness as a 'demonstrable likelihood that the system performs according to designed behavior under a typical set of conditions as evidenced by its characteristics, such as safety, security, privacy, reliability and resilience'.

This definition notably includes the word 'designed', and that implies the specification of requirements, as required by the definition of quality. It is also based on a US National Institute of Science and Technology (NIST) definition (Griffor et al., 2017), and, at the time of writing, the US National Defense Authorization Act of 2020 has just been passed, requiring trustworthy AI based on NIST guidance.

Putting aside the semantic differences in these evolving definitions, developers of AI systems can make a system trustworthy by specifying verifiable quality requirements, with consideration of legal, ethical and social issues. Engineers, be they developers or testers, can build a trustworthy system by implementing and verifying requirements. Stakeholders can then hopefully trust a system because it is objectively trustworthy. Of course, trust is far more subjective than this: people may trust or distrust a system simply because of the brand associated with the company that produces it.

Regardless of the definition of trustworthiness, it is clearly a superset of a particular set of measurable quality characteristics. Researchers have proposed (Kuleshov, 2018) that a functional characteristics vector could be composed of quality measurements, with appropriate weightings, and that this could be compared to standards for particular AI tasks. These standards might contain measurement methods, specific quantities of data involved in evaluation, and the minimum observed quality characteristics allowed for a specific task.

## AI QUALITY PROBLEMS

Artificial intelligence can include symbolic systems, which use knowledge encoded as 'symbols', and sub-symbolic (machine learning) systems, which use previously seen data to make predictions about future data points. Machine learning (ML) is the most popular, and it is difficult to discuss and specify quality goals and analyse how to evaluate it. It is not just quality specialists that think so either, research in Japan involving 278 ML engineers identified the biggest new challenges they face in integrating ML are in decision-making with customers and testing/quality assurance. They identify the lack of a test 'oracle', and underlying imperfection as the top causes of the problems with testing (Ishikawa and Yoshioka, 2019).

An oracle is an abstract concept that helps to solve or just study a decision problem that can be resolved to an answer. Specifically, in systems testing, a test oracle (ISTQB, 2021) is 'a source to determine an expected result to compare with the actual result of the system under test', in order to determine if an individual test has passed or failed.

Symbolic AI does not use ML, but that does not mean it is not a popular method; expert systems can use deduction in combination with explicit rules specified by users or experts. Relatively commonly, search problems, that is, searching through possible solutions to a problem (rather than searching text), use symbolic approaches. These do not suffer from all the same problems as ML, but certainly suffer from some.

Symbolic AI uses symbols and structures, in comparison to sub-symbolic AI (including ML) that uses numeric representations and implicit information encoding (ISO/IEC, 2021a).

So why are there so many problems relating to AI quality? Let us go through them.

### Problem 1. Automation without specification

The first problem is that ML, the most common approach to AI, can also be defined as automation with little or no specification. Rather than specifying logic that describes how a system works, it is trained on datasets. The popularity of this approach largely explains why the use of AI has grown so much in the last two decades, alongside the amount of data that are collected.

An easy-to-understand example of this is recommendation engines used on ecommerce sites. Once you add an item to your basket, it is likely you will see suggestions of other products you may be interested in. Developers are not writing code that identifies related products, rather an ML model can be trained on past combinations of purchases to identify likely candidates to recommend.

> Machine learning is the process of optimising model parameters through computational techniques, such that the model's behaviour reflects the data or experience (ISO/IEC, 2021a).
>
> An ML model is a mathematical construct that generates an inference, or a prediction based on input data (ISO/IEC, 2021a).

So how does this work? Primarily by using neural networks, at least recently. Artificial neural networks (ANNs) are inspired by how the brain works; when we perceive some link between events that occur, our brains send signals down pathways, and the more often those pathways are used, the more powerful those pathways become. ANNs work using similar principles: some experience (training data) is observed, and the greater the correlations between the thing we are trying to predict and particular observable data items (features) are, the stronger those predictive pathways are in the resulting ANN. This means that those same pathways can be used with new, previously unseen data, in order to predict things.

> A neural network (also called an artificial neural network) is a network of two or more layers of neurons, connected by weighted links with adjustable weights, which takes input data and produces an output (ISO/IEC, 2021a).
>
> A neuron is a node in a neural network that takes input values and produces an output value, by combining the input values and applying an activation function to the result (ISO/IEC, 2021a).

There is an intrinsic quality evaluation problem here; if there is less specification needed to produce the system, how will we know it works? It might be intuitive with ecommerce recommendations, but it often is not that obvious with more complex applications. Consider an ML algorithm that recommends news articles that people might be interested in. How do you know that you are recommending the right articles? You might be able to determine if people are clicking on the article, but are you recommending the best one?

## Problem 2. Unknown answers

The second problem is that if we do not know the answer to a particular problem, and we are specifically writing the system to find out the answer that we do not know, how will we know whether it is right?

In the current stage of AI development, this is a problem where AI systems are replacing expert judgement, for example, diagnosing diseases, which takes medical expertise. It is, of course, possible to ask experts to assess if the system is correct, but there are problems with this too. For instance, experts may disagree, and experts may caveat responses in ways that systems cannot. This will be an increasing problem as AI becomes more advanced and begins to solve problems that human experts cannot validate.

Even in terms of verifying the behaviour of simple ML models, this problem manifests in some form. Every ML action is a prediction, for each one of which we need to know the 'ground truth' in order to observe whether the prediction is accurate. This has obvious practical limitations, so evaluation is often limited to a convenience sample.

## Problem 3. Complexity of data

The third problem is the complexity of inputs; say a system has a large range of real-world sensors, how can we predict all the ranges of inputs?

Imagine the complexity of inputs for a self-driving car. One open-source test dataset (Binas et al., 2017) comprising input data that can be used to train self-driving cars, was prepared using a low-resolution camera of just 340 x 260 pixels, to represent the input data from a camera. It also contained data from car controls such as the angle of the steering wheel, the accelerator pedal position and the brake pedal status. Even more data are available about the inner workings of the car such as engine speed, vehicle speed, headlamp status, torque and gear position. Context is also relevant, such as the fuel available and consumed, and the geographical position. Even with the low-resolution camera, 7–10 megabytes of data were recorded every second.

This problem is not unique to AI, but when it is compounded with the data-driven nature of AI, it becomes complex to analyse quality. To explain that another way, a self-driving system that was designed (using explicit logic) to reduce speed when approaching a corner would be verifiable by ensuring that it did that. An ML system that was designed to modify speed based on many hours of training data would be much more challenging to verify. What if it took road conditions or barometer readings into account as well? Or other, less intuitive inputs? What if the expected behaviour was not something as well defined as reducing speed when approaching a corner, but simply mimicking the speed of the drivers in the provided testing and training datasets? In reality, self-driving cars are far more complex than a simple ML model, which leads to the next problem.

## Problem 4. System complexity

AI systems can be very complex. Take for instance a deep learning system; this can be made up of many layers of neural networks, each of which has been created based on training data. The internal structure of these is very complex, but crucially it does not represent the functionality in any way that a human can understand. Conventional systems are more understandable because they contain logic expressed in code that technical people can understand and is logically structured into classes and methods that are essentially defined by a human and usually relate to the requirements, functionality or input and output data in some way.

As well as the complexity of ML models, AI systems often combine multiple models, or combine models with non-ML AI components. The interoperability of these models is important but can be difficult to understand. Wrapping up probabilistic imperfection inside more probabilistic imperfection leads to quality issues that can be difficult to analyse and comprehend.

This complexity also leads to a lack of transparency about how a system reaches a particular decision, which reduces accountability and explainability. This contributes to some of the concerns around truly trustworthy AI.

## Problem 5. Self-optimisation

Another problem to add to our list is understanding how a system optimises itself. How will testing the system change it? How can we understand what has changed? Quality becomes something that evolves as a system adapts.

Some ML systems are trained once, deployed and never revisited. Some are retrained periodically, for example daily, by automating that process. Others use self-learning techniques. An example of this is reinforcement learning, where every action the system takes leads to a 'punishment' or 'reward', and it adapts itself to maximise the reward it can gain.

Reinforcement learning is utilising a reward function to optimise either a policy function or a value function by sequential interaction with an environment (ISO/ IEC, 2021a).

Controlling self-optimisation might be easy to solve if you have complete control of the system and you can specify which interactions are used for optimisation. It might also be easy to restore it to a known state. However, increasingly, organisations are using AI provided as a service by a third party.

I first experienced this testing a cloud-provided natural language processing system. My automated tests first showed some variability; they did not always pass. I could not change the third-party system, but over a period of time my tests started to stabilise – they always worked. I was happy for a while, but then I started to notice that slight variations in the inputs were causing incorrect responses. The model the third-party provider was using was overly optimising to the test inputs I provided, becoming less accurate for general users.

## Problem 6. Human abilities

What if the system is intended to mimic human abilities? How can those human abilities be specified? Try writing a list of quality requirements for a system to be friendly or ethical. You can probably come up with a few ideas, but can you ever consider that list complete? It is unlikely; human behaviour is complex and difficult to express in requirements.

The human brain is an extremely powerful complex system, as is societal behaviour. Properties of human behaviour that we would want AI systems to exhibit, such as ethics, are philosophical in nature and very difficult to specify in terms of desired functionality.

Sebastian Thrun, who founded Google's self-driving car efforts, once said: 'Nobody phrases it this way, but I think that artificial intelligence is almost a humanities discipline. It's really an attempt to understand human intelligence and human cognition' (Thrun, 2018).

The current generation of AI requires either the explicit definition of 'rules', or a lot of examples. It is notoriously bad at generalising outside those rules and examples. This makes it very hard to try to artificially emulate general concepts like human behaviours.

One of the most difficult abilities to specify is ethical behaviour. Ethical theory itself has multiple competing sets of principles. Where an AI system that can render serious consequences to life and liberty in the real world are concerned, ethical decision-making is important, but hard to specify.

## Problem 7. Bias

One of the biggest problems facing AI is that systems usually learn from knowledge provided by humans, and there is usually bias in those data, or even in the requirements. Human cognitive biases, societal and historical biases, data bias and statistical biases are all slightly different and a huge field of study in AI, so much so that a whole chapter of this book is devoted to the topic.

## Problem 8. Drift

Another problem is that the real world is constantly changing. This problem is referred to as concept drift, where the correlation between inputs and outputs changes over time in the real world. Some systems adjust for this, and some systems do not.

Concept drift is where the actual correlation between inputs and outputs changes over time (Google, 2021).

Sometimes the correlations in the real world stay the same, but the observed data change. This is referred to as data drift.

A good example of drift is ML employed to detect fraudulent credit card transactions. Customer habits change, and fraudsters change their attack strategies – this leads to drift in the system (Dal Pozzolo et al., 2015).

This means that quality is a moving target. Imagine how many AI systems continue to predict people would behave as they did before the start of the COVID-19 pandemic. Overnight, predictions would have become invalid, as human behaviour stopped being representative of historical behaviour.

### Problem 9. Automation bias

The last problem is a different kind of bias, called automation bias or complacency bias. What if an AI system is trusted too much, in a way that degrades the quality of the decisions made by humans?

> Automation bias is the propensity for humans to favour suggestions from automated decision-making systems and to ignore contradictory information made without automation, even if it is correct (ISO/IEC, 2021b).

This affects all systems with a human in the loop of decision-making. A high-profile example is the 2018 incident where a pedestrian was tragically killed in an accident involving a self-driving car (Krisher, 2019). The car failed to identify the pedestrian correctly, and the human driver had developed so much trust in the system that they were watching a television show.

In a less high-profile example, many companies now use systems that might extract data from scanned documents or compute data items and display them for an operator to confirm. These systems typically result in a lower quality of human decision-making.

## A MODEL FOR MEASURING AI QUALITY

Quality can, of course, not be quantified with a single metric. It requires the definition of characteristics and terminology that can be used when specifying quality requirements and evaluating them.

ISO/IEC 25010 (ISO/IEC, 2011) is an international standard used frequently for quality management with conventional software quality models, as part of the SQuaRE series of standards. ISO/IEC 25010 has been reviewed by experts and practitioners (Kuwajima and Ishikawa, 2019) who believe it needs to be enhanced to sufficiently describe the quality of AI systems. ISO/IEC plan to extend it to create a new model (ISO/IEC, 2021c), which is likely to be published in 2023.

The product quality characteristics defined in ISO/IEC 25010 are discussed in the rest of this chapter, alongside some discussion on how they might ultimately be extended to cover AI fully.

### Functional suitability

Functional suitability is where most of the focus is placed in quality management, although whether it is the most important quality characteristic is a matter of context. It contains sub-characteristics including completeness, correctness and appropriateness. It measures whether the system has the necessary features and functions.

It can be hard to measure correctness and completeness of AI systems. Where ML is used, a statistical approach needs to be taken. Unlike with conventional systems, it is necessary to consider how frequently the system is wrong, whereas conventional systems are typically working, or not working.

If the data used for testing have the same statistical distribution as the dataset used for training, then it would be expected that an AI system would work correctly. The issues come into play when new and previously unseen data are experienced by the system.

Classification problems are a common application of AI. These problems relate to determining whether something belongs to a particular category. A common example is an image recognition model that determines whether a picture is of a cat. The functional correctness of these systems is usually measured in terms of type I and type II errors. A type I error is a 'false positive', that is, the model incorrectly determines that a picture of a giraffe is a cat. A type II error is a 'false negative', that is, the model incorrectly determines that a picture of a cat is not a cat.

Classification is an ML function that predicts the output class for a given input (ISO/IEC, 2020).

Regression problems are where the output of the model is a number. Measuring the correctness of a number requires different measures such as measuring the average error, which is the average distance between the correct number and the number the model calculated (known as the mean absolute error). There are lots of other measures that can be used though, as the mean absolute error gives no indication about the directionality of performance.

Regression is an ML function that outputs continuous (typically, floating point) values.

A very important topic in the context of functional correctness is bias. Bias is a complex and overloaded term that is used differently by different people. It is common for data scientists to describe bias as a statistical concept that can be positive or negative in any given context, but philosophers, policy-makers and ethicists may think of bias as something that leads to unfairness in outcomes. In an AI system it is both: it relates to the data and an algorithm, but it is also cognitive. Cognitive biases can exist in the team that creates the system; for example, a team may use stereotypes about other people, or groups of people, in deciding the function of a model. A belief that a human has may not be accurate, but the development of the model may propagate that belief if the developers optimise the model to confirm it.

Another way models can be biased is through the sources of data used to train the model, for example there are many times more pictures of white westerners than others on the internet. Training a model based on pictures of people taken from the internet would therefore be more accurate in any function that involved white westerners. Firms that seriously engage with producing high-quality facial recognition must invest significant effort in compensating for this.

Bias is an accuracy issue that can be measured in the same way as general accuracy is measured but grouping the results by particular groups (demographic or otherwise) allows for comparison between the results for everything, and the results for these groups. Other measures are required when assessing ranked outputs, but the principle of comparing the group under analysis to the general population remains.

## Context coverage and completeness

The environments and expected inputs and outputs are more limited with conventional systems. For example, consider a simple chatbot. The whole point of a chatbot is that it is expected to be able to process the English language correctly. In a limited context, such as providing support for a single product, it might be quite effective at answering questions. However, the range of inputs it may receive can vary significantly and it is impossible for developers to anticipate all the possible inputs.

The degree to which an AI system can process the inputs required speaks to the systems coverage of the relevant context, and its completeness. In fact, this is one of the largest and most important areas of AI research. How can a system that works well in one context be transferred to a completely different context and still function correctly? This is the difference between the 'narrow' AI in use today, and the artificial general intelligence expected in the future.

> Artificial general intelligence (or strong AI) is generally understood to be the point where AI can gain equivalent intelligence to humankind.

Context coverage can also be described as the ability to maintain performance with previously unseen datasets or inputs. There is a complex relationship between this and bias. The greater the flexibility of a system in different contexts, the greater the risk of bias.

## Flexibility and adaptability

Adaptability is defined as a product quality sub-characteristic in ISO/IEC 25010, as the 'degree to which a product or system can effectively and efficiently be adapted for different or evolving hardware, software or other operational or usage environments' (ISO/IEC, 2011). It is currently part of the portability characteristic, but the way we describe it in the context of AI is more functional. Traditionally, this is understood to relate to the environment that the system works in (be it an operating system, supporting software environment or hardware). However, AI systems can change in real time with reinforcement learning, or after models have been retrained with new data.

Adaptability of an AI system can also be measured as the time taken for a system to react differently based on a change in observed data, or how easily it can be retrained.

## Robustness

The environment in which an AI operates might change naturally, for example through drift in the correlations between inputs and outputs. It might also change through malicious activities. Robustness describes the extent to which an AI system will maintain performance as the environment changes. This is different from context completeness; however, it is to some extent captured within the term 'context coverage'. Making AI systems robust, particularly to malicious attacks, requires solutions to some very difficult problems.

Attacks on AI systems have a relatively long history; attempts to bypass spam filters are an early example (Grosse et al., 2017). More recently, deep neural networks have started to add such complexity to AI systems that it is very difficult to identify ways that the system can be fooled.

Computer vision systems can be fed slightly changed images; just a few pixels can be changed and a picture of one person can be made to look like another person to the machine, in a way that would not fool a human (Kurakin et al., 2017).

Adversarial attacks are where an attacker slightly perturbs (changes) the inputs to a model in order to influence its prediction(s) (ISO/IEC, 2021a).

New ways to trick AI systems are being found all the time, including natural language systems (Alzantot et al., 2018), where words are added to text without changing the meaning, but changing the result of the AI system.

## Transparency and explainability

Transparency and explainability are huge issues with AI systems, and there are multiple concepts tied up within these. One issue is the degree to which a user or other stakeholder can comprehend the reasons for an AI system's outputs. This is usually referred to as explainability. However, transparency is a wider topic than explainability. For a system to be transparent it is necessary to understand the source and quality of input data, including labels, annotations and rules.

One researcher, Creel (2020), describes transparency in three different ways:

- **Functional transparency**. The availability of information about the whole operation of the system.
- **Structural transparency**. The availability of information about the implementation.
- **Run transparency**. The availability of information about how the system was run in a particular case.

Functional transparency suggests that a stakeholder can understand the system well enough to predict how it will behave in a particular case. This is possible with conventional systems, as you can follow the explicit logic in code. With complex algorithms comprising layers of neural networks and multiple interacting AI components, it can become nearly impossible.

Structural transparency might be obtained by understanding the code, algorithm and training data. With this transparency, statistical analysis can be performed on the training data to reduce concerns about accuracy and bias.

Run transparency is the same as explainability. Researchers (Arya et al., 2019) have explained that there is a difference between a directly interpretable system that is intrinsically understood by users, and a system that would require an activity to be performed to obtain an explanation of a specific prediction. They also discuss interactive explainability, where users can drill-down and interrogate systems about decisions. One example envisaged in the context of robotics is a button on a robot that triggers the robot to explain its last action.

Whatever the method used, explainability can be measured in terms of the availability of an explanation, the accuracy of the explanation and the time in which an operator is able to obtain (and possibly communicate) an explanation.

## Societal and ethical risk mitigation

AI systems usually intend to treat everyone differently – that is part of their purpose – but this is also why there is a risk of ethical issues. We have already discussed issues relating to bias in AI systems, which can result from propagating existing unfairness in society, or can relate to unfair outcomes resulting from system implementation.

Unfairness is difficult to measure and varies wildly between contexts and cultures.

Freedom from risk measures assess the degree that the quality of the AI system mitigates potential risk to users, organisations and the wider community. The traditional quality models focus more on health, safety and the environment; however, for AI systems it is also relevant to consider the risks to the rights and freedoms of members of society.

Measures for health and safety, for example, usually relate to reported injuries or hazards. With AI systems, unfairness might not be reported unless there are public investigations. One example of this is the 2016 ProPublica (Larson et al., 2016) investigation into the parole systems used in the United States. Researchers analysed an algorithm used to determine whether a prisoner would be likely to reoffend, based on various data items, but not including race. The research found that black offenders were far more likely to be predicted to reoffend, due to societal bias inherent in the data. That is, a higher proportion of black people committed offences, therefore the system was more likely to predict them to reoffend. Despite race not being recorded, other variables (such as postal code) often correlate with race.

Bias is not the only way that ethical risk mitigation needs to be considered. One very popular discussion is the 'trolley problem'. This is a popular thought experiment (Wikipedia, 2020) that can be applied to self-driving cars. If a car identifies that a collision is inevitable, and any action will result in a fatality, who should die? This may include the driver (and the owner of the system), and multiple different pedestrians. How should the system make a decision? What is fair in this context?

## Controllability

The degree to which a system can be controlled is not a new concept (PK et al., 2021), and is usually a functional characteristic of a system. Nevertheless, AI systems are increasingly able to operate autonomously without needing human intervention or control. If human interaction becomes optional or impossible, we need to consider how controllable an AI system is for its human operators or users.

Controllability might be the ability to move a system from a particular initial state, into another state, through a control function (such as a button on the back of a robot). The quality of this process might relate to the number of steps the operator has to perform, the reliability of the outcome and how long a system takes to move between states.

> **Quality in use**
>
> ISO/IEC 25010 defines two models, a product quality model and quality-in-use model. The first is typically considered to be the quality of a system at the point of release, and the second is the quality of the system in actual use.
>
> Some of the issues discussed in this chapter span both the product quality of the system and the quality in use. This is because of the problems referred to earlier when discussing context coverage, for example deploying a system trained on faces in one country, into another country, can lead to widely different outcomes.

## REGULATION OF AI QUALITY

Quality is not normally a regulated aspect of systems, except in specific areas, usually safety critical ones. However, due to the increasing use of AI in systems that make decisions about people, various regulations have come into force, or are progressing, that legally constrain organisations about quality.

Some of these specifically relate to the use of personal data in algorithms (Chaudhuri et al., 2018).

### The General Data Protection Regulation (GDPR)

The GDPR (European Parliament, 2016) requires that risks arising from the use of personal data in systems that make some automated decisions are mitigated. This surprises some people, but a key principle of data protection is ensuring that the data held about people are in fact correct. When AI is used to process personal data, for instance for clustering users into different types, that inference can also become personal data. Accuracy in data protection also relates to the output of AI systems, for example if they are making any kind of automated decision about people.

The opening sentence of Article 22 of the GDPR reads: 'The data subject shall have the right not to be subject to a decision based solely on automated processing, including profiling, which produces legal effects concerning him or her or similarly significantly affects him or her.' It then lists some exceptions and some mechanisms that can be used; however, a key part of complying with the Article is ensuring the principle of accuracy remains.

## The proposed EU AI regulations

So, while the GDPR provides some regulation on automated decision-making, it does not specifically talk about AI. After signposting the need for better regulation for some time, at the time of writing, the European Parliament is considering a proposed EU AI Regulation (European Parliament, 2021). If this is passed, it will be a wide-reaching legislative change. It will probably be the most significant cross-sector regulation to affect testing and quality management for many years.

While the detail of the regulation will evolve, the initial text prohibits certain uses of AI, such as social scoring and subliminal manipulation. For others, such as employment-related systems, it deems them high risk and places obligations on organisations to establish a technical quality management system. In this section we will explore the scope and likely requirements for such systems.

Firstly, the definition of AI is notable for its breadth. It does not only regulate ML, but more symbolic AI techniques and, surprisingly, any statistical technique. That could potentially mean that spreadsheets that use average values could fall inside the technical scope. Many will think that is too broad, but others will say that the quality issues affecting ML (e.g. bias) can manifest in those statistical techniques to the same degree.

As an example of this, during the COVID-19 pandemic in 2020, many students were unable to sit exams. The UK government introduced a system (BCS, 2020b) that would predict the result of the exam a student was not going to sit, and that would become their final grade. The calculations were based on the historical performance of the school, the specific subject at the school, the ranking of the students by the teachers and their teacher-predicted grades.

The algorithm usually gave weight in particular to the rankings performed by teachers and applied that against the historical spread of results from that subject, and school. That meant that the algorithmically predicted grade was often very different from the teacher-predicted grade, leading to many unhappy students. In addition, where the number of people studying a subject was small, it instead relied more on the teacher-predicted grade instead of the teacher's ranking. This caused controversy as particular types of schools offered a greater diversity of subjects with smaller class sizes. These schools, being more expensive, tended to ask weaker students to leave rather than allowing them to continue, and were less likely to be attended by certain groups in society. It was widely perceived that the more expensive the school you attended, the better the grades allocated by the algorithm for students. The public outcry was significant, the algorithm was abandoned, and the head of the relevant government department resigned.

This is arguably not an example of an AI system, but it is an example of how using statistical techniques can lead to many of the issues discussed in this book. It is also an example of a high-risk use case as defined in the AI Regulations, alongside creditworthiness assessment, or recruitment use cases. It is reasonable to assume that statistical techniques are used in most creditworthiness assessments, and ML is starting to be used in recruitment.

The proposed regulations do not prohibit these use cases, but they focus on establishing a regulatory ecosystem for managing them, a set of controls that must be established, and large fines for non-compliance.

The regulation puts an obligation on the developers of AI systems to ensure that they are appropriately accurate, robust and secure. The level of accuracy that is determined by testing, and the specific metrics used, need to be determined. They also need to be resilient to failures, whether caused by functional or non-functional faults. With regard to security, data poisoning attacks are specifically mentioned. This is where an attacker is able to poison the training data, or other input data, in order to influence the predictions made by the system.

The controls are the most interesting part for us, as they focus on two things, the identification and management of risks, and the quality management and testing activities that must be performed.

They require things such as representative test data, ongoing production monitoring and significant amounts of documentation relating to testing. They put specific requirements on the testing, and in some cases will even require independent audit of training and test data, code and test results. They also require that statements about accuracy (presumably obtained from the test results) need to be provided to deployers of third-party systems. All of this testing will result in a CE mark – a quality mark heavily used in Europe for everything from cosmetics to furniture – that permits sale, import and export of products.

If you are outside the EU and working with AI, the regulations will affect you, as it is 'extraterritorial' in scope, like the GDPR. That means that it applies to any system that may affect EU citizens – not just those systems developed in the EU.

The problem with the draft legislation is that detailed techniques for many of the required control and testing objectives are in their infancy. Best practices are still evolving, and international standards are some way off. As an example, we know we can measure neuron coverage rather than code coverage with neural networks, but the research on the effectiveness of this technique is in its infancy.

The International Software Testing Qualifications Board (ISTQB) has released a specialist certification scheme for AI Testing, which is going to be a great step forward. However, it will likely need to be updated to take into account the EU view as it evolves over the coming months and years. It is worth noting that we have some time; much like GDPR, it is expected that there will be a long implementation period as the details are figured out. Final implementation is likely to occur in 2023 or 2024.

## SUMMARY

In summary, there are a range of quality considerations that apply uniquely to AI systems. Terminology and models are still evolving, and regulatory pressure looks likely to force increasing focus on AI and quality over the coming years. One of the most important concerns that spans these areas is bias, which we will dig deeper into in the next chapter.

# 3  QUALITY AND BIAS

## James Harold Davenport

It is common to accuse systems, particularly AI systems or systems incorporating AI, of being 'biased' or 'unfair'. These two words are often used synonymously, but we will follow the International Organization for Standardization (ISO) paradigm and distinguish between them – 'bias' being a statistical phenomenon, capable of precise definition, and 'fairness' an ethics one, whose interpretation depends on, for example, 'established norms', and hence perceptions of fairness can vary. More precisely, we adopt the following based on work under way in ISO/IEC SC 42, one of the standards development organisations examining the issue:

'Bias' is a systematic difference in treatment of certain objects, people, or groups in comparison to others (ISO/IEC, 2021a, Definition 3.2.2; ISO/IEC, 2021b).

'Fairness' is treatment, behaviour, or outcomes that respect established facts, beliefs, and norms and are not determined or affected by favouritism or unjust discrimination (ISO/IEC, 2022).

This is an important distinction, often lost in the noise of marketing and politics. For example, Facebook have a tool called 'Fairness Flow', trumpeted as 'How we're using Fairness Flow to help build AI that works better for everyone' (Kloumann and Tanner, 2021). However, the technical description is much more modest (or 'realistic' if one prefers):

> Fairness Flow is a technical toolkit that enables our teams to analyze how some types of AI models and labels perform across different groups. Fairness Flow is a diagnostic tool, so it cannot resolve fairness concerns on its own — that would require input from ethicists and other stakeholders, as well as context-specific research. However, Fairness Flow can provide necessary insight to help us understand how some systems in our products perform across user groups (Kloumann and Tanner, 2021).

There is an interesting contrast here: this message mentions stakeholders, but then asks about performance across user groups, not wider stakeholders: see the section 'Targeted advertising is biased' later in this chapter. In fact, neither are really a correct description. If we ask Fairness Flow about gender bias in automated hiring tools, we are probably interested, not in gender bias with respect to the user (the human resources operative), but with respect to the data subject (the person being considered for hiring).

In this chapter we will look at some of the basic statistics underpinning the definition of bias, and some examples of bias, both intended and unintended, in everyday life. One example will be gender-biased car insurance pricing, where the raw data show a bias (men have more, and worse, accidents), and then the question is whether taking this difference into account in pricing is fair.

## CONSEQUENCES OF THE BIAS DEFINITION

There are various consequences of measuring performance across user groups:

(i) We need to have a set of decisions to look at: we cannot say of a single decision in isolation 'that decision was biased'.

(ii) We need to have at least two sets of objects, people or groups, such that we can say 'These treatments were biased in favour of A rather than B.'

(iii) We need to know which differences in treatments were applied to each set.

(iv) The sets need to be large enough that it is feasible to have unbiased, or at least less biased, decisions. For example, if we are choosing one individual out of many (e.g. a recruitment panel), then the decision is biased in favour of every group to which the selected individual belongs (this is also an example of consequence (i)). Equally, if we are choosing ten individuals out of a thousand, these decisions are bound to be biased (either in favour or against, depending on whether or not we select from that category) with respect to every category with less than a hundred members in that population of a thousand.

In practice we also need the sets, and the amount of bias, to be large enough that the amount of bias is unlikely to have arisen by chance. Let us suppose we have populations consisting of equal numbers of A and B, and that we have a picking system that does not differentiate between members of A and members of B (that it is unbiased between A and B). A statistician would say that we have the **null hypothesis**, that there is no difference between A and B as far as this system is concerned. Let us take a look at the probability of our system picking different numbers of members from different population sizes:

- **Picking two members out of a population of four**. Here the chance of picking the two A members is one-sixth (because the chance of picking an A the first time is one-half, and there are then one A and two B left, so the chance of picking a second A is one-third). The same for two B members and picking one of each class (AB or BA) has a probability of two-thirds.

- **Picking three members out of a population of six**. Here the chance of AAA is one-twentieth, as is BBB, and AAB and ABB each have chance nine-twentieths.

- **Picking four members out of a population of eight**. Here the chance of AAAA (or BBBB) is one-seventieth, AAAB (or BBBA) is eight-thirty-fifths and AABB is eighteen-thirty-fifths.

- **Picking five members out of a population of ten**. Here the chance of AAAAA (or BBBBB) is 1 in 252; AAAAB (or BBBBA) is 25 in 252, and AAABB (or BBBAA) is 100 in 252.

- **Picking 10 members out of a population of 20**. The probabilities are now 1/184,756 ≈ 0.0000054, 25/46,189 ≈ 0.00054, 2,025/184,756 ≈ 0.011, 3,600/46,189 ≈ 0.078, 11,025/46,189 ≈ 0.24, 15,876/46,189 ≈ 0.34 for an even split, and then the same in reverse.
- **Picking 50 members out of a population of 100**. Here the chance of an **exactly** even split is roughly 5 per cent, and all other probabilities are less, so we cannot even expect an unbiased system to give us a perfectly unbiased answer.

Statisticians are used to this problem, and approach it by asking not what the probability of an exact value is, but what the probability of seeing at least (or at most) this value is. More formally, suppose $T$ is the value we are observing (in our case the number of A chosen). Then we ask, for a threshold value $t$, 'what is the probability that $T > t$ under the null hypothesis' (assuming that we are interested in the question 'are too many A being chosen?'). If we are observing an event $t$ such that this probability is very small, then we can conclude:

**Either:** the null hypothesis is false (in our case the picking system is differentiating between A and B).

**Or:** we have observed an unlikely event.

A statistician chooses some significance level $\alpha$, observes $t$, calculates the probability $p$ that $T > t$ under the null hypothesis (what is the probability that I would have seen something at least this surprising?) and compares $p$ with $\alpha$. If $p$ is smaller, then the usual jargon is that the statistician 'rejects the null hypothesis' but note that this does not mean the null hypothesis is false, as we could always have observed an unlikely event.

This brings us to the key question: what should $\alpha$ be? A common value in science is $\alpha = 0.05$, but this should be associated with the conclusion 'further experiments are required': one-twentieth isn't that improbable. Other common values are 0.01 or 0.001, but much smaller values are also used. For example, the Higgs boson discovery (CMS Collaboration, 2012) was announced with $\alpha = 1/3,500,000$ (this value is $5\sigma$ from statistical theory) and the accepted standard in genome analysis (G. M. Clarke et al., 2011) is $5 \times 10^{-8}$ (1 in 20 million).

There are two warning notes that should be sounded.

We have been talking about a single direction of bias (choosing A over B). However, there can be many possible directions, and they may not be binary. For example, the UK's Equality Act 2010 defines nine protected characteristics, and while a few are binary, many, such as age, are not. Even if they were all binary, and if our system were unbiased, while the chance of failing a given one of them at the $\alpha = 0.05$ is, by definition, one-twentieth, the chance of failing one of nine at that level is 37 per cent. Hence, it is quite likely that a simplistic test will declare that a system that is in fact unbiased is biased according to one of these characteristics. That is, **if** we perform the experiments first **then** choose the characteristic. A simple solution to this is known as the Bonferroni–Dunn correction (Bonferroni, 1936; Dunn, 1961) and replaces $\alpha$ by $\alpha^* = \alpha/n$ if we have $n$ different directions of bias. A slightly more subtle correction is the Šidak correction (Šidak, 1968), with $\alpha^* = 1 - (1 - \alpha)^{1/n}$, but the difference is very small in practice, and a statistician should probably be consulted if the difference matters. Hence we should be looking at $\alpha^*$ being 0.0056 (or 0.0057 if using the Šidak version) for each of nine directions of bias, if we are to have a 0.05 chance of declaring an unbiased system to be possibly biased.

These are tests for **statistical** significance, not practical significance. The distinction is especially important in medicine, where the phrase 'clinical significance' is used to indicate that the effect actually matters.

## BIAS IN EVERYDAY LIFE

Life as we encounter it is actually full of biases: some explicit and some implicit, some human-constructed and some not. An example of a human-constructed explicit sex bias was the male-preference primogeniture rule (until 2015) that the eldest **male** child inherited the throne of the UK, with a female child only inheriting if there were no male children. Historically there were very many such explicit human-created sex biases, and while many have been legally abolished, their effects linger. To continue the example, male-preference primogeniture means that choosing a random monarch of the UK is much more likely (thirteen-sixteenths, excluding 'William and Mary') to choose a king than a queen.

Another bias, seemingly created by nature, is that women tend to live longer than men. This is true even if we set aside issues such as war, which tend to kill young men. Life expectancy at 65 in the UK shows that women can expect to live two years longer than men, on average (Institute and Faculty of Actuaries, 2018). For centuries, insurance companies and annuity providers have dealt with this by quoting different rates for men and women, with the intention of unbiasing the expected payout. However, this approach has been ruled illegal in the European Union ('Test-Achats Ruling') (European Court of Justice, 2011) and all insurance rates must be quoted without bias for gender. This means that the rates are unbiased, but the payouts are now biased – a woman can expect to receive more than a man. This is an example of a general principle: **where there is a bias due to nature, we cannot remove it, only change where it shows up.**

In many societies, but certainly in the UK, men, particularly young men, have more, and worse, road traffic accidents than women. *The Guardian* newspaper (2004) notes that men are guilty of causing 94 per cent of the accidents involving death or bodily harm. Hence insurance companies used to quote higher premiums for male drivers. Again, this is now illegal in the European Union. However, other factors, such as car type and driver's occupation, can be used. This was studied in the context of the UK car insurance market by McDonald (2015). He observed that the ruling was effective in eliminating direct gender discrimination. However, in the UK, many occupations have a strong gender bias – among his examples were plasterer (96 per cent male) and dental nurse (100 per cent female). Indeed, he found dental nurses were being charged 9 per cent less than the average for car insurance, and plasterers 9 per cent more.

The conclusions of McDonald require careful interpretation.

> It is found that the Ruling has been effective at stopping direct discrimination by gender. However, for young drivers, for whom the difference in risk between males and females is greatest, there is evidence that firms are engaging in indirect discrimination using occupations as a proxy for gender, with insurance prices becoming relatively lower (higher) for those in female (male) dominated jobs. The implications of this go beyond the motor insurance market as it is possible that this could also be observed in other markets affected by the Ruling, for example pension annuities.

The last sentence is certainly true and has significant implications. In reading the earlier sentences, we must be careful not to anthropomorphise. These prices come out of a comparison website that is interrogating the pricing engines of the various insurance companies. No human being is engaged in the detailed pricing decisions: they are reached on the basis of a large amount of data analysis. Indeed, these analysis programs may well not have been changed (the author has been informed that in at least one case they were not), just the variables being input had 'gender' removed. A common phrase would be 'occupation is a proxy for gender', but again this is anthropomorphic: what is happening is that the statistical engines are simply computing correlations, or one might say 'following the data'.

## Differential pricing is intrinsically biased

The car insurance example above illustrates a general fact that many people try to ignore: all differential pricing is biased; and it is biased against those who are charged more. The question is not whether it is biased, the question is whether the bias is acceptable, socially or legally. Gender-biased car insurance was socially acceptable for many years in the EU (and indeed probably still is, despite not being legally acceptable) and is both socially and legally acceptable in many parts of the world today.

An example of differential pricing is train fares. In the UK we are used to paying very different prices depending on whether we are travelling 'off-peak':[1] for example, a return from Bath Spa to London varies (at the time of writing) from £214.20 ('peak'), via £86.80 ('off-peak'), to £63.00 ('super off-peak'). While there are complaints about the absolute amount, and the size of the differential, the existence of the differential is very largely unquestioned. The same is very largely true of airline fares, but these depend on many more variables, and are not as regulated, so the effect is harder to measure.

However, there is much anger when the same principle is applied to holidays and the relationship with school term and holiday dates: *The Telegraph* newspaper (Spocchia and Morris, 2020) talks about 'The "daylight" robbery' of school holiday price increases', and many other similar articles can be found. In fact, the price differential quoted, 'nearly three times', is less than the train fare differential, but the public anger is far greater.

These are all examples of **a priori** pricing: the customer knows in advance what is being charged and, subject to other constraints such as work commitments or school

---

1   But not in many countries. A similar trip (Heidelberg to Frankfurt) in Germany varies from €17.90 to €28.90 but depending on the type of train rather than the time of day, and indeed the €17.90 trains seem to be the fastest.

holidays, can choose to pay less by buying a different service. A classic example of **a posteriori** pricing, where the service is bought first, and then the price established, is a taxi fare. For a conventional metered taxi, the price is determined as a **published** function of the **a posteriori** meter readings (distance travelled and time waiting) and various published parameters, generally time of day and day of week or holiday status. However, for services such as Uber and Lyft, the pricing is more dynamic (akin to airline prices). This was investigated by Pandey and Caliskan (2020), and the results popularised by Lu (2020). They specifically analysed ride-hailing in Chicago, and their

> results indicate that fares increase for neighborhoods with a lower percentage of people above 40, a lower percentage of below median house price homes, a lower percentage of individuals with a high-school diploma or less, or a higher percentage of non-white individuals.

The last is a protected characteristic, and discrimination here may be illegal. Looking at their maps for the first three characteristics, it is clear that these three characteristics are quite correlated, as might seem reasonable. We do not have the corresponding map for ethnicity, alas, and it would be interesting to know how correlated this is.

This is not the only instance of racial bias appearing in what one would naively expect to be an unbiased demand pricing algorithm. Angwin et al. (2015) report that the price charged by the Princeton Review for its online SAT tutoring services vary by ZIP code, from (in 2015) $6,600 to $8,400. They discovered that:

> Asians are almost twice as likely to be offered a higher price than non-Asians. The gap remains even for Asians in lower income neighbourhoods. Consider a ZIP code in Flushing, a neighbourhood in Queens, New York. Asians make up 70.5 percent of the population in this ZIP code. According to the U.S. Census, the median household income in the ZIP code, $41,884, is lower than most, yet The Princeton Review customers there are quoted the highest price.

The student who originally discovered this price differential has a key point. 'It's something that makes a very small impact on one individual's life but can make a big impact to large groups' (Angwin et al., 2015). This is an important point: if one ethnic group is disproportionately priced out of educational support, there will be a knock-on effect on educational disparities.

**Targeted advertising is biased**

This is a blindingly obvious statement when one thinks about it: targeting is biasing by choice. Consider placing advertisements in magazines: a manufacturer of combine harvesters is more likely to advertise in *Cereals Weekly* than in *Interior Decorators Weekly*. Few people would object to this, and indeed the readers of *Interior Decorators Weekly* would probably object to a lot of combine harvester advertisements. However, an advertiser for something else, say jobs as a COVID-19 vaccination site assistant, would be as likely to advertise in one as the other.

However, online advertisement targeting, as practised by Facebook in particular, but also by many others, is different. Rather than being driven by explicit choices, such as subscribing to *Cereals Weekly*, it is driven by the agency's (Facebook, etc.) desire for profit, which is generally obtained by people clicking on the advertisement. Hence the agency would be likely to place advertisements for combine harvesters next to stories about cereal prices and so on. However, there are not that many of those, so the agency is likely to put the advertisements in front of readers whose behaviour, as tracked by, say, the Facebook pixel (Newberry, 2019; Venkatadri et al., 2018), indicates that they might be interested in combine harvesters.

If we were merely interested in combine harvester sales, this wouldn't matter so much. However, one of the things advertised on social media is housing, a subject that is protected from racial discrimination under United States law. There were many issues with social media permitting targeted advertisements, but the major firm involved has agreed to prevent such explicit targeting by the advertisers (ACLU, 2019). However, that is not sufficient to avoid bias, as discovered by Ali et al. (2019). The same mechanism that places combine harvester advertisements in front of people likely to buy them (as perceived by the systems) will also place advertisements for houses to buy (rather than rent) preferentially in front of white people, for example.

Another socially relevant commodity advertised on social media is jobs. This has been investigated by Ali et al. (2019), and more recently by Imana et al. (2021). They point out that, under United States law, 'ads may be targeted based on qualifications, but not on protected categories'. It is not clear whether it is legal to target based on likely interest: naively one might expect advertisements for combine harvester operators to follow the same principles as combine harvesters, and certainly the magazine advertiser would be more likely to use *Cereals Weekly* than *Interior Decorators Weekly*.

Their methodology (Imana et al., 2021) was to place 'two concurrent ads for similar jobs, but for a pair of companies with different de facto gender distributions of employees'. Their conclusion is especially interesting as it illustrates that bias by gender need not be inherent in these processes.

> We confirm skew by gender in ad delivery on Facebook, and show that it cannot be justified by differences in qualifications. We fail to find skew in ad delivery on LinkedIn.

As with Princeton Review pricing, the impact on society is much more significant than the impact on individuals, as we see the perpetuation of gender imbalances.

All of this says that the biases we may be aiming for (e.g. safer drivers) are possibly correlated with biases we are not aiming for (e.g. gender), and we are possibly not allowed to have. In this case, we have a choice between not aiming for the original bias (unlikely in the case of an insurance company), or deliberately correcting for the unwanted consequential bias. However, such corrections may actually be illegal, as discussed for lending in the United States (Hao, 2019), or impossible, as it may be illegal to collect the necessary data (e.g. collecting racial data in France).

In the days of manual CV processing and shortlisting, it was common for personnel departments (as 'human resources' was then called) to have a separate sheet with demographic data, with the statement that these would not go to the short-listing panel, but only be used for bias monitoring. This mechanism is obsolete, and it is not clear that people would have the same faith in a fully automated process as they used to have in the paper processing. However, the spirit needs to be remembered, and unwanted bias needs to be checked for, rather than just assumed not to exist.

## UNINTENDED BIAS

We may be building our AI systems for certain kinds of bias (qualifications, etc.), and we may have corrected for any consequential biases, but other kinds can creep in. There are many causes of this.

### Data bias

The data we have may well not be representative of the full range of circumstances in the real world. Indeed, they cannot be completely representative unless the entire world is included in the dataset, so the usual hope is that we have a 'representative subset'. There are many variants of data bias, currently being enumerated by ISO/IEC with a detailed report: ISO/IEC TR 24027 (ISO/IEC, 2021b). A very important one is sampling bias, which occurs when the dataset sampled is not representative of the demographics or other important features of the real world. As is well-known to pollsters, people chosen at random are not generally representative: it depends on the method of choice, and on the willingness of people to answer questions.

Collecting large amounts of data is extremely expensive, especially if the data need to be labelled. Hence there is a great tendency to rely on 'well-known' datasets. Despite being 'well-known', these themselves may not be representative: Shankar et al. ( 2017) report that, *for the images they were able to acquire location data for* (22 per cent for OpenImages, and a somewhat lower fraction for ImageNet, and with some possibility of error), OpenImages is sourced 32.1 per cent from the United States and 12.9 per cent from the United Kingdom (a total of 45 per cent), and ImageNet is 45.4 per cent from the United States and 7.6 per cent from the United Kingdom (a total of 53 per cent). The top 14 countries, based on average ranking (note that the top 14 countries are identical in the two datasets) are given in Table 3.1, where we have added Wikipedia's population rank: only 6 of these 14 are in the population rank top 14: conspicuous by their absence are Indonesia and Pakistan (4 and 5 in Wikipedia's table).

There are many other useful examples in this paper: one study they did looked at the likelihood that images of 'bridegroom' would be correctly classified. Not surprisingly (given Table 3.1) images from the USA (and from Australia) were much more likely to be correctly classified than images from Ethiopia or Pakistan. This, and other similar observations, has led to the 'Datasheets for datasets' movement (Gebru et al., 2021): 'By analogy [with electronic component datasheets] we propose that every dataset be accompanied with a datasheet that documents its motivation, composition, collection process, recommended uses, and so on'.

Many other 'well-known' data sets contain errors as well, for example the Inside Airbnb dataset (Alsudais, 2021). But the problems with ImageNet are particularly insidious because of the wide use of ImageNet as a starting point. 'This practice of first training a CNN to perform image classification on ImageNet (i.e. pre-training) and then adapting these features for a new target task (i.e. fine-tuning) has become the de facto standard for solving a wide range of computer vision problems' (Huh et al., 2016). There is therefore a risk that errors and biases in ImageNet (or other starting points) could persist through the 'fine-tuning', even if the fine-tuning data were perfect. That this is not a purely theoretical risk is shown by Steed and Caliskan (2021). They have many findings, but one is this: 'Both iGPT and SimCLRv2 embeddings [pretrained on ImageNet] also associate white people with tools and black people with weapons in both classical and modernized versions of the Weapon IAT [Implicit Association Test]'.

**Table 3.1 Country of origin of images** (Source: Shankar et al., 2017)

| Country | ImageNet | | OpenImages | | Average | | Wikipedia population rank |
|---------|------|------|------|------|------|------|------|
| | % | Rank | % | Rank | % | Rank | |
| USA | 45.43 | 1 | 32.10 | 1 | 38.76 | 1 | 3 |
| UK | 7.58 | 2 | 12.90 | 2 | 10.24 | 2 | 21 |
| Italy | 6.23 | 3 | 2.75 | 9 | 4.49 | 3 | 25 |
| Canada | 3.01 | 4 | 3.73 | 5 | 3.37 | 4 | 37 |
| Spain | 2.46 | 6 | 4.09 | 4 | 3.27 | 5 | 30 |
| France | 2.06 | 8 | 4.29 | 3 | 3.18 | 6 | 20 |
| Australia | 2.80 | 5 | 2.88 | 8 | 2.84 | 7 | 53 |
| Germany | 1.63 | 9 | 3.16 | 6 | 2.40 | 8 | 19 |
| Japan | 1.18 | 11 | 2.96 | 7 | 2.07 | 9 | 11 |
| India | 2.08 | 7 | 1.52 | 11 | 1.80 | 10 | 2 |
| Brazil | 0.96 | 14 | 2.03 | 10 | 1.49 | 11 | 6 |
| Netherlands | 1.40 | 9 | 1.47 | 12 | 1.44 | 12 | 67 |
| Mexico | 1.11 | 12 | 1.09 | 13 | 1.10 | 13 | 10 |
| China | 1.05 | 13 | 1.00 | 14 | 1.03 | 14 | 1 |

## Historical bias

All data collected are clearly data from the past. How far into the past is generally unknown, and indeed many internet resources are not clearly dated. We saw one example earlier when we looked at the gender of monarchs of the United Kingdom, but there are many others.

This problem of the persistence of the past, and the stereotypes of the past, or indeed the stereotypes of the present, bedevils language processing in particular, as pointed out by Caliskan et al. (2017). Their example is Google's translating of Turkish (a language with gender-neutral pronouns) into English (a language with gendered pronouns), so that 'O bir doktor. O bir hemşire' becomes 'He is a doctor. She is a nurse' has been 'fixed' to 'She is a doctor. She is a nurse' (after a transitional period in which the user got a dialogue about gender-neutral pronouns). However, the trivial (to a human) change to 'O bir matematikçi. O bir hemşire' gives 'He's a mathematician. She is a nurse'. The same problem can arise with gendered nouns: the Romanian words 'profesor' and 'profesoara' are translated into English as 'professor' and 'teacher' respectively. It should be noted that there is no simple solution to these problems: good language translation is a skilled business requiring, at times, large amounts of context.

## Labelling bias

Many applications require labelled data, generally labelled by humans, and there can be errors or human bias (see below) introduced in the labelling process. One might hope that errors were small and not systematic, but this needs to be verified rather than assumed. The labelling process may also introduce systematic errors. The ProPublica study referred to on page 19 also pointed out (Angwin et al., 2016) the confusion in US bail software between three concepts:

  (i) 'Has reoffended', which is unmeasurable, since not all offences are resolved, but which is the desired metric, and, worse, what the software was described as using.

 (ii) 'Has been convicted of re-offending', which is subject to bias in the policing system, and may or may not be corrected by the judicial system. Most people probably assumed this was what the software was using, since it is what human judges use.

(iii) 'Has been accused of re-offending', which is also subject to bias in the policing system, and was actually used.

There are complex sociological and methodological questions here, not least that an offender who has been refused bail is very unlikely to re-offend while locked up. So we cannot measure the 'false positives', that is, people who were refused bail, but who would not have been accused of re-offending if bail had been allowed. A simpler example of label confusion is in the account (Perry, 2019) of bicycle counting in San Diego, which was meant to count cyclists, but also counted bicycles hanging on the back of cars.

## Data processing bias

The processing of data, and ML typically has a complicated pipeline of data processing, may introduce errors. Real-world data tend to contain gaps, or 'missing values' as statisticians tend to refer to them. A trivial example, which the author uncovered many years ago, consisted of coding Male=1, Female=2, Unknown=9, and then taking averages. This led to incorrect statements about the gender mix of the samples, only spotted when there were enough 'Unknown' to make the average 2.1, and the researcher sought the author's help with this 'bug'. With a complex pipeline, and many actors involved in the data pipeline, more subtle variants of this can slip through.

## Human bias

Humans are biased, whether consciously or unconsciously (Gilvoich and Griffin, 2010). These biases may act in the present, or may have acted in the past, to mean that past data, which are what ML algorithms often rely on to predict the future, are biased. This shows up in employment hiring (Bertrand and Mullainathan, 2004; Stokel-Walker, 2021), and indicates that we should be especially careful of these applications.

Accommodation is another area where discrimination may be illegal in many places, and is in Oregon (Serrano, 2022). However, at least some of the discrimination is computing (not specifically AI)-enabled human discrimination, as reported in Edelman et al. (2016). Since an Airbnb host has more information than would normally be available for a hotel booking, they can also be more discriminatory: 'requests from guests with distinctively African-American names are roughly 16% less likely to be accepted than identical guests with distinctively white names'. Their conclusion is worth noting: 'On the whole, our analysis suggests a need for caution: while information facilitates transactions, it also facilitates discrimination'.

While many explanations can be given for human bias, such as general bias, group attribution bias, implicit bias, confirmation bias, in-group bias, out-group homogeneity bias, 'What you see is all there is' bias and societal bias, the key point is that 'real-world' data may well be biased.

## SIMPSON'S PARADOX

'Simpson's paradox' is a phenomenon where the trend in separate groups can disappear, or even be reversed, when the groups are combined. Though it had been noted earlier in the history of statistics, this paradox is normally attributed to Simpson (1951), who made a more systematic study of it. A simple example can be seen in Figure 3.1.

**Figure 3.1 Simple illustration of Simpson's paradox**

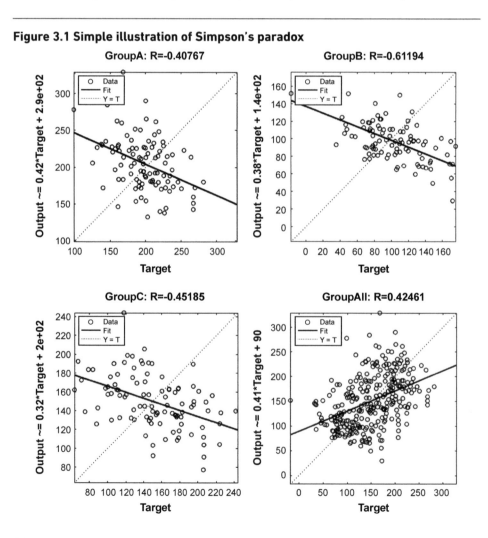

Here we see that in all three Groups, taken individually, the Output is a decreasing function of the Target (with a slope of about −0.4), but across the union of all three groups, it's an increasing function (with a slope of about +0.4). These data, and more examples, can be found at https://doi.org/10.15125/BATH-01099 (Davenport, in press).

An important example of the paradox is given in Simpson's paper. Consider first a researcher who is wondering whether the ratio of court to plain cards in a normal (French-suited) pack of 52 cards is different between black and red cards. However, some cards are dirty and some clean, which the researcher also records in case it matters. The researcher records Table 3.2.

**Table 3.2 Cards by colour and cleanliness** (Source: Simpson, 1951 © 1951 Royal Statistical Society)

|       | Dirty |       | Clean |        |
| ----- | ----- | ----- | ----- | ------ |
|       | Court | Plain | Court | Plain  |
| Red   | 4/52  | 8/52  | 2/52  | 12/52  |
| Black | 3/52  | 5/52  | 3/52  | 15/52  |

Among the dirty cards, 4/7=57 per cent of the court cards are red, but 8/13=61 per cent of the plain cards are red. Hence the dirty plain cards are more likely to be red than the dirty court cards. Among the clean cards, 2/5=40 per cent of the court cards are red, but 12/27=44 per cent of the plain cards are red. Hence, the clean plain cards are more likely to be red than the clean court cards.

But if we ignore the dirty/clean distinction, we get Table 3.3 for a standard (French-suited, 52-card) pack of cards. There is no distinction between red and black: both have 20/26=77 per cent plain.

**Table 3.3 Cards by colour** (Source: Simpson, 1951 © 1951 Royal Statistical Society)

|       | Court | Plain |
| ----- | ----- | ----- |
| Red   | 6     | 20    |
| Black | 6     | 20    |

The apparent conclusion is obvious: we should ignore the clean/dirty distinction.

Now consider Table 3.4.

Among the men, 4/7=57 per cent of the untreated survive, but 8/13=61 per cent of the treated survive. Hence the treated men are more likely to survive. Among the women, 2/5=40 per cent of the untreated survive, but 12/27=44 per cent of the treated survive. Hence the treated women are more likely to survive. Surely the conclusion is that the treatment is good. However, numerically, Table 3.4 is identical to Table 3.2, just with different labels, and if we combine male and female, we will get Table 3.3 again, and observe that there is no difference between treated and untreated, so the treatment might appear valueless. As Simpson says, 'The treatment can hardly be rejected as valueless when it is beneficial when applied to males and to females.' An approximate explanation of the paradox in this setting is that we treated a far greater proportion (27/32=84 per cent) of women than men (13/20=65 per cent), but women are more likely to die (18/32=56 per cent) than men (8/20=40 per cent) and we should have done a balanced experiment.

**Table 3.4 Survival by gender and treatment status** (Source: Simpson, 1951 © 1951 Royal Statistical Society)

|  | **Male** | | **Female** | |
| --- | --- | --- | --- | --- |
|  | Untreated | Treated | Untreated | Treated |
| Alive | 4/52 | 8/52 | 2/52 | 12/52 |
| Dead | 3/52 | 5/52 | 3/52 | 15/52 |

A potentially serious case of Simpson's paradox in the real world is described by Bickel et al. (1975). They looked at admission to graduate study at the University of California, Berkeley, in fall 1973. Their first analysis looked like Table 3.5.

**Table 3.5 Admission to University of California in fall 1973**

|  | **Observed data** | | **Expected if no gender bias** | |
| --- | --- | --- | --- | --- |
|  | Admit | Deny | Admit | Deny |
| Men | 3738 | 4704 | 3460.7 | 4981.3 |
| Women | 1494 | 2827 | 1771.3 | 2549.7 |

This shows that, while the overall acceptance rate was 41 per cent, it was 44.3 per cent for men and 34.6 per cent for women, and a statistician would do a $\chi^2$ test and conclude that the probability of this occurring by chance was vanishingly small. However, at Berkeley, the decision to admit is made by the individual departments, who have widely differing admission ratios and widely differing gender ratios among the applicants. Furthermore, the two are correlated: 'The proportion of women applicants tends to be high in departments that are hard to get into and low in those that are easy to get into.' In fact, a more detailed analysis shows that there is a bias *in favour* of women admitted. As the authors conclude: 'The bias in the aggregated data stems not from any pattern of discrimination on the part of admissions committees, which seem quite fair on the whole, but apparently from prior screening at earlier levels of the educational system.'

## SUMMARY

The first conclusion is that bias-free AI is pointless: we *want* AI to treat some groups differently from others, that is, to be biased in favour of those groups, since there is no point in using it unless it makes distinctions. However, we want it to make the *right* distinctions, and there may well be ethical or legal requirements that AI does not have certain biases (e.g. gender, ethnicity, ability). This may actually be a very difficult, or impossible, job: in the case of young drivers it is impossible to be fully biased against accident-prone individuals without being gender-biased in many cultures. However, we can make some comments we hope will be helpful:

(i) 'I don't collect gender (or ethnicity or …) so I cannot be biased about it' isn't true. There are a vast number of proxy variables, as the car insurance saga (McDonald, 2015) shows. Indeed, if you do not collect gender (or ethnicity or …), all you can say is that you do not know whether you are biased or not. It is unlikely that Uber and Lyft set out to be racially biased in Chicago (Pandey and Caliskan, 2021), or that the Princeton Review set out to be racially discriminatory in its pricing (Angwin et al., 2015), but all of them turned out to be.

(ii) Natural biases may be impossible to eliminate and can only be moved. So, the Test-Achats ruling, in requiring annuity rates to be unbiased, introduced the corresponding bias into annuity payouts.

(iii) Care in data selection is important, even though it too is not a guarantee. Having more data may simply mean that you have a greater manifestation of the existing bias in society (Metz, 2019).

(iv) It is important to be honest about what the labels on your data actually *are*, as opposed to what you would like them to represent.

(v) Be careful with 'missing values' and other anomalies in the data.

(vi) As shown in the Berkeley case, looking at summary statistics can be very misleading, and as Bickel et al. (1975) conclude: 'If prejudicial treatment is to be minimized, it must first be located accurately.'

All data created during this research are openly available from the University of Bath Research Data Archive at https://doi.org/10.15125/BATH-01099

# 4    TESTING MACHINE LEARNING SYSTEMS

## Adam Leon Smith

In this chapter we will explore testing ML systems, how testing specialists fit in to the process, levels of testing, metrics and techniques. In addition, we'll discuss how to test some specific characteristics of AI systems.

### THE ROLE OF A TESTER

If you are working in an organisation developing ML systems, you might be lucky enough to be working with a smart team of data scientists and engineers. Some testing and quality specialists (as well as developers, for that matter) might be intimidated by the mathematical-sounding language and seemingly magic processes these teams use. Frequently, testers shy away from fully testing their outputs, or are discouraged from evaluating them. How can someone without data science expertise find holes in work by specialists?

There is no reason why the work would not be full of defects. Data scientists are no better at finding issues with their models than developers are at finding issues with their code. Conventional developers miss issues in their own work because of confirmation bias, that is, because they are making assumptions, or they inject small logical errors into their work. Data scientists also make assumptions. Sometimes these assumptions are based on their expectations of the predictions the model should make, rather than reality. It is too easy to keep tweaking the hyper-parameters of a model until you get the results you expect to see, without considering whether those results are correct.

Hyper-parameter is a variable set by a human in an ML model, before training the model.

The first area where testing and quality specialists can add value is simply by asking the right questions. Two of the most important qualities they can have are, firstly, thinking critically about the work outputs and, secondly, being fantastic at spotting risks. This starts at data collection and labelling. How have data for training been gathered? Are they representative of the real-world distribution? How have they been labelled? Have sample checks been carried out on the labels? What are the motivations of the labellers? Are there any subsets of the training data that might have been labelled incorrectly? Just asking these questions can reveal root causes of potential faults that may otherwise not be detected until much, much later.

Some of these questions can be explored statistically. For those with some technical skills, it might be useful to load the training data into an exploratory analysis tool (this might be a spreadsheet, a Python library or an off-the-shelf business intelligence tool). You can explore the data yourself and look for outliers, patterns, inconsistencies, sampling issues and errors.

The next area to look at is the data pipeline, which is the process by which data get to and from the model. Perhaps your organisation has a skilled data engineering team that takes the data scientists' requirements and builds a great data pipeline that transforms and manipulates the data, or perhaps the data scientists build it themselves. The latter is a red flag for quality; data scientists are not engineers, and data pipelines are an engineering output. The code quality of data pipelines can be terrible, for this reason (Lenarduzzi et al., 2021). Component testing code coverage is of course the first place to look, but do not be surprised if there is very little.

A data pipeline is the infrastructure supporting an ML algorithm. It includes acquiring data, pre-processing and preparation, training one or more models and exporting the models to production.

Where data pipelines are built by separate teams, there is of course a risk of assumptions and implementation constraints being overlooked. The end-to-end integration between the source of the data, and the predictions from a model are crucial. You might hear that the data scientists have tested a million records in their model, but most likely those records have been fed in using CSV or some other format directly to the model, skipping the end-to-end data flow. Consider some potential bugs that might slip into the integration.

Firstly, the data pipeline could erroneously transform certain values that are features of the model, leading to incorrect predictions for both affected and unaffected records. For example, age could incorrectly be transformed to a single digit, leading to highly incorrect predictions if age was a key component of the prediction.

Secondly, the data pipeline could pass null values for some fields incorrectly, and that leads to the entire record being dropped. ML does not work well with missing values, resulting in incorrect training and missing outputs. For example, a lookup based on postal code could fail and leave city as a null, resulting in a failure to consider that record valid in either training or operation.

Thirdly, the data pipeline could duplicate some records incorrectly, and that would create too many examples of the duplicated record, skewing the model towards the values in those records.

A key role of a tester is identifying the scope of and approach for testing at each test level, with specified components and acceptance criteria. It is important that the product risks that emerge from an integrated system and the ML model are identified appropriately and mitigated through testing.

## THE NATURE OF ML

We have discussed some of the quality problems AI can have, but there is one problem that turns testing very much on its head. ML uses statistical correlations to make predictions, and this is both its super-power and its weakness. As outlined before, this allows 'automation without specification', and allows for predictions to be created without human engineers really understanding the patterns that a model is identifying and using to make those predictions.

Conventional software is largely deterministic (if we forget about small differences introduced by things like multi-threading) and uses explicit logic to determine outputs. We can look at a specification, design some inputs and usually predict the outputs or actions of a system. With ML, that is much harder. It can be hard because it is too difficult to calculate the expected outcome, but it can also be hard because we do not expect ML systems to have 100 per cent accuracy.

For example, think about a facial recognition system. We can perhaps take 100 photographs of people's faces, knowing that those faces are known to the system, and run them through the system as a test. Now, if 99 of those faces are recognised, but one is not, is that a test failure? It is unclear. This is an example of a test oracle problem.

It may also be of questionable validity because 100 is not a statistically significant number in the context of the global population of faces. Often, we really need to be testing thousands (or more) sets of inputs to get something that is statistically meaningful. Further, while with facial recognition we can use our human eyes to try to determine the expected results (a match, or not a match), with many predictive systems it is not that easy to determine the 'ground truth'.

It is also difficult to use white-box testing techniques (that is, with knowledge of the code or structure of the system) because the internal structure of the ML model is not easily understood. Conventional software suffers from defects that follow certain heuristics (loop boundaries, field boundaries, field combinations), and this has led to testing techniques designed to detect such defects. Even when we are black-box testing a system (that is, without knowledge of the internal structure), we can use these techniques to find likely issues. ML largely does not follow those heuristics, so it is more difficult to plan tests that will expose issues. For all we know, our facial recognition system may completely fail with types of faces that are different in ways the human eye struggles to perceive.

ML can be described as a probabilistic system. A probabilistic system is one that is difficult to describe without using probability. For example, the weather is a probabilistic system as it is too difficult to model every particle, every gust of wind, and every temperature variation at a micro-level. So, forecasters use probability to make predictions. ML models are in many ways similar.

These testing problems are not insurmountable, but they require a different mindset from testing conventional software. They can also be significantly compounded by several factors. One of these is the integration of multiple ML components to create an integrated system. This is more common that you may think; for example in facial recognition it is common to use one model to detect the face within a larger image, and one to perform the identification against an existing dataset of face images. When you combine multiple probabilistic systems together, it becomes harder to predict behaviour, and in turn, predict what might go wrong.

Another problem is the use of 'AI-as-a-service'. Much like software-as-a-service, this abstracts a lot of the complexity away into a third-party application programming interface (API) that is called to deliver the predictions. This can save a lot of effort on the development, but from a testing perspective it can be a nightmare. It makes the system less transparent, and usually makes testing it at a statistically significant scale more difficult. Instead of a data scientist running millions of records through the model on their desktop, you need to dynamically call APIs to get results.

Throughout this book you will see reference to test oracles. An oracle is something that allows you to determine whether a test has passed or failed. These might be requirements, specifications, alternative systems (pseudo-oracles) or just things you know (implicit oracles).

## Levels of testing

A test level is a specific instantiation of a testing process. In a conventional project this will typically first comprise component testing that tests the smallest independent module of software, then integration and system testing and acceptance testing. Dependent upon the context, technology, risk and methodology being used, these levels vary from project to project. In highly iterative and agile projects these levels are executed in small increments, over a short period of time.

So how does this change with ML systems? From one perspective, not a lot. The levels of testing remain broadly the same; however, more careful thought might need to be put into the planning simply because of the complexity of the technology. To explain this, it is first necessary to consider why we have such levels in the first place – essentially, because it is easier to find and investigate failures when the verification scope is smaller. To illustrate this, consider a boundary (or 'off-by-one') error in a simple for loop in a micro-service. To find and detect this in a system or acceptance testing process, when many components have been joined together in an integrated system, is very complex. The effort involved to run end-to-end tests covering a boundary value is likely to be significant. The effort required to investigate the resulting failure and pin it down to the root cause is also going to be significant. Contrast this to a component test, where writing a test to check a boundary is almost intuitive, and the cause of the failure is likely to be faster to find.

We can apply the same logic to detecting failures in the predictions of an ML model. It is far easier to find and detect that failure when running a large volume of tests in a model testing process, than in an integrated, costly end-to-end environment. It is necessary to plan testing to ensure that complex failures are detected as early as possible, without introducing additional unnecessary components.

From another perspective, there are two test levels that are quite different from a conventional test process: model testing and input data testing. The first has already been mentioned: model testing is a form of component testing but can be clearly contrasted from conventional component testing. It is statistical in nature, it involves large amounts of data, the test results are complex and require mathematical analysis, and it is an iterative process normally conducted by a data scientist.

Typically, a data scientist will receive a dataset for training and testing a model. Some proportion of those data (between 20 per cent and 40 per cent, normally) will be held back for validation. The remainder will be used for training the model. To put this another way, most of the data are shown to the ML model as examples, the remainder are used to check that the model behaves correctly. There are several complexities here, for example for some methodologies a data scientist can dynamically attempt training using different subsets of the data for testing, and thereby provide multiple levels of testing with different subsets. This helps to ensure that the model is not overfitting to a particular training dataset.

This test level is critical, and it is not something a testing professional should be trying to pull away from a data scientist; it is effectively part of the development process (much like test-driven development at the component test level). However, there are three pitfalls to be aware of. The first is experimenter's bias. This is a human cognitive bias that occurs when the experimenter (in our case, the data scientist) has a preconceived notion of what the test results of the model should be and fails to notice a flaw in their methodology because the results confirm their expectations. An example is failing to notice that the dataset that they have been provided with only contains a limited set of examples from some arbitrary subset; that means the population of data is not representative of reality. For this reason, it is useful to do some input data testing (more on this later).

The second pitfall is to assume that because the model has been thoroughly tested in this way, high-volume testing of the functional performance of the model is not required in later phases. This is not the case. In almost all ML implementations there is a complex data pipeline that pre-processes and adapts the data ready for testing. This might comprise adjusting images from cameras by normalising contrast or might involve transforming structured data values. These data pipelines carry all the same risks as conventional software, and by simply accidentally dropping some records, or incorrectly transforming some values, the effect on the ML predictions at a statistical level can be dramatic. It is necessary to thoroughly test the end-to-end data flows, and statistically test the overall system in later stages.

The third pitfall is not actually doing model testing at all. This is unlikely to happen where an in-house developer is developing a model, but can often occur where a software developer leverages a third-party model, or third-party model hidden behind a web-service facade. AI-as-a-service is an increasingly common business model, where ML components are leveraged without in-house data science skills. In this example it is crucial that model testing is carried out, and it may fall to quality and testing professionals to flag up this risk.

Going back to input data testing, this can be considered a test level. It falls into the category of static testing (that is, testing without dynamically executing a program), and is sometimes called 'exploratory data analysis' (Figure 4.1). Generally, it would take the form of obtaining the training data for an ML model and analysing the statistical properties of them.

---

**Figure 4.1 Exploratory data analysis and model testing scope**

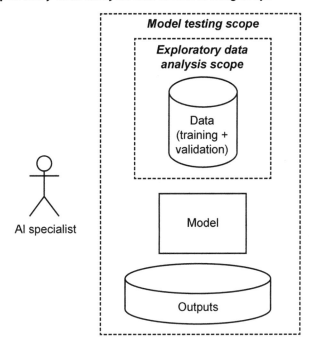

There are several reasons for doing this. Firstly, one of the biggest causes of ML prediction failures is imbalance in the training dataset. Analysing the distribution of data can reveal imbalances. For example, consider non-response bias, that is, where certain people tend not to answer questions or surveys. You might find that data are skewed towards groups of people who have more time or inclination to provide data. Another example is facial recognition; many models are trained based on publicly available data on the internet, which are skewed towards white male westerners. Detecting such an imbalance in training data allows you to detect likely failures (and bias) in trained models.

Another example of an issue you might detect in input data testing are partial data. ML models do not work well with partial data. Let us say for example we have some structured data with three columns, but one column is optional. Typically, a data scientist will either impute (guess) the missing values or drop the rows where that column is missing. Even if you start with a reasonably balanced dataset, the process of dropping some of the records can introduce an imbalance.

Although it is not a test level, it is normal to conduct far more monitoring of an ML system's functional performance on an ongoing basis. Typically, with conventional software we build it, test it, then throw it over the wall into 'production', or live usage. We tend not to frequently revisit it. However, with ML systems we need to continually review and revisit the quality of the system in live usage. There are a few different reasons for this. Firstly, the quality of ML is wholly dependent on how well the training data represent the 'unseen' data it will encounter in the live environment, so it is necessary to continue monitoring the data after go-live to ensure that the model remains robust. In addition, models can suffer from concept drift, that is, the correlations between inputs and outputs that are presumed to exist (because they exist in the training data) are not static, they change over time. Consider a model designed to predict foot traffic in a shopping mall based on various datasets. No doubt as soon as the COVID-19 pandemic occurred the correlations between different input features and shopping mall foot traffic were turned on their head. This is an extreme example, but as the real world changes, the quality of ML model predictions can both improve and degrade. Another reason for monitoring the quality of ML in production is bias detection; it can be difficult to determine bias sometimes in a test environment, again due to a potential difference between the training data and the data a model is exposed to in the live environment, and continued monitoring can help with this.

In summary, there are two specific 'levels' of testing that are not likely to be required (or at least, as important) with conventional software that we need to consider in relation to ML: model testing and input data testing. However, more testing may be required on an ongoing basis.

User acceptance testing of AI systems, while broadly the same as conventional user acceptance testing, may need additional focus. It could be that the system is designed to replace human activity, in which case it might be necessary to compare the behaviour of a system to humans. Special consideration should be given to automation bias, that is, the degree to which human decisions degrade when supported by a machine, or when monitoring a machine.

## TESTING METRICS

Testing processes are frequently measured, either as part of a management and control process, or as part of an exercise to understand the degree to which the testing 'covers' the basis of testing. The latter is discussed in the next section. There are lots of other metrics that can be applied to testing ML systems, often in terms of their accuracy, or performance. These are used because we do not expect ML to get everything right all the time, so we need to run a statistically significant number of tests and look at the test results statistically too. This is like analysing the results of performance testing (how fast something runs under a certain load of data or users).

There is an important terminology difference between the software engineering and the AI/ML domain in the way the word **performance** is used. For some reason, engineers use 'performance' to mean time-behaviour, efficiency and resource utilisation. Not so in AI/ML, where 'performance' simply means how well the system or model behaves given a *particular metric*. To try to avoid confusion, we use the term 'functional performance'.

The functional performance of an ML model is measured differently depending upon the business objectives, and the type of output. Two of the most common types of output are a continuous number or prediction of whether something belongs to a particular class. As you can imagine, these are quite different types of output, which we discuss in different ways.

Regression models, in ML, are those that output a continuous variable, that is, a floating point number. Classification models are those that predict whether something belongs to a particular class.

For regression model results, we can use mean square error (MSE). That is simply the average error rate (the difference between the expected value and the predicted value) squared. If I run 10 tests and the expected result should be 0 for each test, and all the actual results are 10, then my (mean) average error is 10. However, if the actual results range between −10 and +10, then my simple average might end up being 0, indicating incorrectly that all my tests pass. That is why we 'square' the error; as you can see in Table 4.1, it more correctly reflects the result:

**Table 4.1 Example of MSE**

| Expected result | Actual result | Error | Squared error |
|---|---|---|---|
| 0 | −10 | −10 | 100 |
| 0 | 0 | 0 | 0 |
| 0 | +10 | 10 | 100 |
| | **Average:** | **0** | **66.66** |

For measuring the results of classification models, we need to take a different approach. Each prediction has two properties, whether the prediction was that something did or did not belong to a class, and whether that prediction was correct. These are referred to as true positives (correctly predicting something belongs to a class), true negatives (correctly predicting something does not belong to a class), false positives (incorrectly predicting something belongs to a class) and false negatives (incorrectly predicting something does not belong to a class). Not only does this mean we have two separate modes of failure, but the impact of those failures may be very different. Predicting someone has a disease, incorrectly, has a very different impact from incorrectly predicting someone does not have the same disease. In the former, they may find out through follow-up tests and predictions. In the latter they may not get tested again.[1]

We therefore often visualise these failure rates through a confusion matrix (it is perhaps called a confusion matrix because although it originated in the study of statistics, it was used for many years primarily in the study of psychology). Figure 4.2 is an example of a confusion matrix.

**Figure 4.2 A confusion matrix**

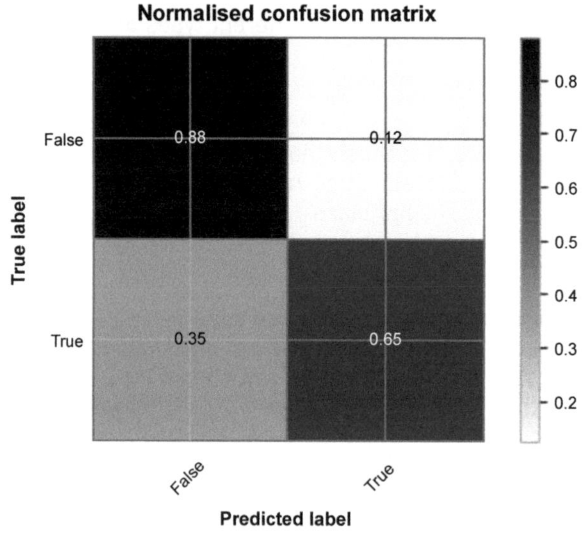

**Normalised confusion matrix**

## TESTING TECHNIQUES

The 10 tests used as an example for MSE in the previous section are unlikely to be enough to get statistically significant results. That of course leads to the question 'How many does?' Well, much like in the testing of conventional systems, exhaustive testing is not possible. Conventionally we use a risk-based approach combined with test techniques shown to maximise the likelihood of finding an error, by exploiting heuristics of common software errors. We prioritise requirements and analyse the structure of the system to design test procedures that contain expected results.

However, where the system is non-deterministic, there may be multiple valid outputs from the system's processing – even when presented with the same inputs and starting from the same state.

So how can we approach this challenge with ML? There are several ways, none of which is fundamentally proven yet to be the best approach, but that is also partly true of

---

1    Even though such false positives can be resolved through further testing, the impact of false positives over a large population can still lead to millions of people being given an incorrect positive result with a significant impact.

conventional test techniques. In fact, focusing on any one test technique too much can lead to problems like test case explosion, so they should always be used with care and in a balanced way.

## Combinatorial testing

In some circumstances, you can analyse the data that have been used for testing, against all possible variations of input data. Given the ML model is trained to respond to input data, looking at the variety of input data used can give you a proxy for coverage. For example, if you have 'age' or 'country' as an input feature, you can look at whether the test data have covered all ages and countries to a statistically significant degree. This might be useful, but it might also be a lot of effort to obtain or manufacture additional data. It is also a technique that is only applicable to the simplest use cases. Imagine trying to do this with facial recognition; the sheer volume and variety of inputs is staggering.

One way to simplify the selection of test inputs is to use the concept of pairwise testing. Pairwise testing (or All-pairs testing; Wikipedia, 2021) is based on the concept that manipulating pairs of inputs exposes more defects than simply manipulating a single input. It is based on research conducted on conventional software (Nie and Leung, 2011), but that does not mean it does not apply to ML.

To apply pairwise testing, we can take a variety of inputs. With facial recognition as an example, we could use skin colour, eye colour, nose size, background and lighting. We can assume that each of these inputs can be bucketed into 10 possible values. For instance, using equivalence partitioning you might bucket lighting into 1–10, where 10 represents very bright, and 1 represents very dark. After applying buckets to each input, you are left with 5 inputs with 10 possible values, that is 50 test cases for each input, and $50^5$ possible test cases, or 312 million. Applying a pairwise technique to these will reduce the number of test cases to just 100. Explaining the mathematics of this is somewhat outside the scope of this book, but there are plenty of online resources, papers and even web-based test design tools you can explore to investigate this technique further.

Using this technique does not alleviate problems you may have with your test oracle, that is, challenges determining whether a test has passed or failed.

## Neuron coverage

Test coverage is a widely discussed concept in software engineering. At one end of the spectrum, test analysts might map requirements and business processes to sets of tests, to measure the degree to which the high-level business requirements have been covered by tests. At the other end of the spectrum, in automated testing (particularly in component testing), it is common to measure the statements and branches of code in the software under test that have been covered by those tests. This is performed by instrumenting the code (or using a wrapper around a Java Virtual Machine) and leads to a scientific measure of test coverage. In fact, this is required for some domains, such as the safety testing of road vehicle systems.

How can we do this with neural networks? Firstly, we need to drill a little more into the detail of how neural networks work. Before that we need to recap on Boolean logic.

Boolean logic is the foundation of computer science, it is how we process 1s and 0s (binary numbers) inside hardware processors and low-level machine code. The most important Boolean operators are OR, AND, NOT and XOR.

- If I pass two binary numbers to an OR operator, it will return 1 if either input is 1 and 0 if neither is.

- If I pass two binary numbers to an AND operator, it will return 1 if both inputs are 1, and 0 if they are not.

- If I pass one binary number to a NOT operator, it will return the other binary number (i.e. if I pass 0 it will return 1, and vice versa).

- If I pass two binary numbers to an XOR operator, it will return 1 if either input is 1, and 0 if they are both 0 or both 1.

Without dwelling too much on how these powerful but simple concepts underpin modern computing, let us look at how we could replicate the AND operator using a really simple neural network.

A layer of a neural network comprises two important variables, weights (one per input) and an activation value. The weights determine the relative importance of each input to the layer, and the activation value determines the decision boundary for the output. The training process automatically determines the correct weights and activation values based on the training data and the model hyper-parameters.

The mathematics of a neural network layer can be described as follows:

$$y = 1 \ if \ \sum_{i=1}^{n} wi * xi + w0 \geq \theta$$

To break that down a bit:

- $y$ is the output value.

- $xi$ represents all our inputs, in the AND example there are two inputs $x1$ and $x2$.

- $wi$ represents our weights, which are both 1 in the AND example, as both inputs have equivalent importance.

- $w0$ represents a constant value (of our choosing).

- $\theta$ represents the activation value (the decision boundary), usually values less than zero output a zero, and values of zero and greater return one.

Breaking the above formula down into manageable chunks, first we need to multiply each input by its associated weight, then add the results together ($\alpha$), as shown in Table 4.2.

We know that the AND operator should only return 1 if both inputs are 1, and from Table 4.2 we can observe that $\alpha$ is clearly different in this scenario: it is 2. In order for the result of our formula to be 1 only in this scenario, we need to adjust $\alpha$ so that it is the only result greater than or equal to zero. We do this by adjusting the constant $w0$. In this example we can set it to −1.5, and now we have the AND operator implemented in a neural network as shown in Table 4.3.

**Table 4.2 Initial example of the AND operator as an activation function**

| x1 | x2 | w1 | w2 | x1 * w1 | x2 * w2 | a = (x1 * w1) + (x2 * w2) |
|----|----|----|----|---------|---------|---------------------------|
| 0 | 0 | 1 | 1 | 0 | 0 | 0 |
| 0 | 1 | 1 | 1 | 0 | 1 | 1 |
| 1 | 0 | 1 | 1 | 1 | 0 | 1 |
| 1 | 1 | 1 | 1 | 1 | 1 | 2 |

**Table 4.3 Example of the AND operator as an activation function**

| x1 | x2 | a = (x1 * w1) + (x2 * w2) | a − w0 | Y (a − w0≥0) |
|----|----|--------------------------|--------|--------------|
| 0 | 0 | 0 | −1.5 | 0 |
| 0 | 1 | 1 | −0.5 | 0 |
| 1 | 0 | 1 | −0.5 | 0 |
| 1 | 1 | 2 | 0.5 | 1 |

Obviously, this is an incredibly simple piece of logic to try to replicate. Also, a data scientist would certainly not train a neural network by developing lots of tables and analysing the data at this level, they would simply train the model by providing examples, and the ML framework would make all the necessary adjustments to weights and constants. In practice, multiple layers are required to interact with each other in order to solve most problems.

Going back to test coverage, even though ML models are ultimately machine code, it is not going to be relevant to apply traditional code coverage measures such as statement coverage. This is because the same lines of code are usually run for each prediction. We need to adjust the measures to handle the formula described above. These measures are built around the following questions:

- Has a test caused every neuron to achieve an activation value of greater than 0?

- Has a test caused every neuron to achieve both a positive and negative activation value?

- Has each neuron been covered by two tests with a certain distance between activation values?

- Have pairs of neurons in adjacent layers been tested in combination, so that the change in the activation value in the first layer causes a change in the activation value in the second layer?

Bear in mind that measuring neuron coverage helps you to understand how much of your model is exercised by your tests, but it does not tell you the expected results of those tests or tell you whether you are checking the right things. Also, tools for measuring these coverage criteria are not widely available, and require testability features to be added to the ML framework.

## Experience-based testing

Exploratory testing techniques can be applied to ML, as can checklist-based techniques. Much like error guessing techniques can be used to guess where bugs might be in conventional software, the same can be applied to ML.

Experience-based testing uses implicit oracles, either heuristics related to quality risks discussed in the previous chapter, or standardised checks.

For example, when performing experience-based input data testing, one might ask:

(i) Is there a protected category variable in the features?

(ii) Is there another feature that correlates with a protected category variable?

(iii) Is there less than a representative amount of data associated with a protected category variable?

Another example of a checklist-based technique is using Google's list of 28 ML checks to determine readiness for production (Breck et al., 2017). This includes checks on the feature selection, the architecture, the documentation and the test results.

Some researchers (Herbold and Haar, 2022) also found that by using conventional test techniques, such as boundary value analysis, they were able to find fundamental defects in ML frameworks themselves. For example, by passing '0' for many features they were able to cause the framework to crash.

## Metamorphic testing

Metamorphic testing is a test technique that generates new test cases from previous test executions. It is unusual as a test technique in this regard, as usually tests can be designed in advance of executing them. In some ways, it is a little like exploratory testing using an implied oracle, as the tester establishes some heuristic and uses that to determine expected results. In exploratory testing such an implied oracle might be 'the result of a square root should never be negative'. In metamorphic testing it might be that the model should provide fewer results if more inputs are provided, or be more likely to predict something, given a particular input. These heuristics are called metamorphic relations, and they establish a probabilistic relative requirement upon the system and allow us to create expected results for follow-up tests.

A simple way to imagine such a test is any online store where you can filter items in a search. A search with a filter should, generally, give fewer results than a search without a filter. By executing a series of test cases, you can gradually apply filters and see fewer results. While you cannot easily predict how many results you will see each time, you can see whether the metamorphic relation holds true.

Metamorphic testing can be useful when you are having trouble determining the expected result of a test in advance. Again, an oracle problem.

## A/B testing

A/B testing is a technique where two variations of a system are used, and the results compared. This technique takes its name from a marketing technique, where small variations in marketing emails or on websites are presented to different groups of users to see if it changes their responses.

A/B testing can be used to test two models and can be particularly useful where the 'ground truth' is not known. Consider for example where you are recommending news articles of interest to individual users; how do you know that you are recommending things that they are actually interested in? One way is to monitor what they click on and compare the click-through-rate from results provided by two models.

## Use of experts

Some test oracle problems can be alleviated using experts to help determine if a test passed or failed. Consider a system that replaces those with expertise in a field like diagnostic medicine; at some point, during the testing, it is essential to have some medical diagnostic experts in the room.

There are challenges with the use of experts: they naturally vary in competence and they may disagree. Humans can express things with ambiguity or adapt their responses to add caveats. This is more difficult for an expert system to do.

Experts may also have particular motivations about automation; it might be necessary to make evaluations double-blind, so experts do not know whether they are reviewing the outputs of a colleague or a machine.

## Adversarial testing

Models may be vulnerable to adversarial attacks. Adversarial testing is testing a model to learn about the model's behaviour and then to identify potential vulnerabilities. It is exactly what an attacker would do, but with different goals – to prevent the attacks.

Adversarial testing may also involve the use of tools to conduct white-box analysis on the model to identify successful adversarial attacks and add them to the training dataset to make the model less vulnerable to them. However, this is not how an attacker would do it. An attacker would rely on the fact that most of these vulnerabilities are actually transferable models, so they might try to build a similar model, find vulnerabilities in that and then try applying them to the model they are trying to subvert.

Adversarial testing can be considered both a functional and a security test, in that it is simulating attacks that are trying to change the functionality. As mentioned in Chapter 2, adversarial examples can be found in multiple types of application of AI, including computer vision and natural language processing. In both cases, the overall image or text is still seen to be conveying the same information to a human, but is perceived differently by AI.

## Back-to-back testing

Back-to-back testing, also called parallel or difference testing, helps where there is an oracle problem. An existing or otherwise alternative implementation is used as a reference, or a pseudo-oracle.

Any tests that are run on the system under test can also be run on the alternative implementation and the results compared. This approach has been used for a long time in testing, for example in financial services where the results of two large batch systems that perform millions of calculations can be compared, without the intellectual activity of defining the expected result for each calculation.

One way to do this is to use industry standard ML benchmarks, which represent a certain level of functional performance. These benchmarks might be labelled, and therefore allow for the functional performance of the system to be tested without a test oracle; however, it is necessary to consider how that labelling occurred. A study in 2021 found a 3.4 per cent label error rate across popular benchmarks (Northcutt et al., 2021).

## TESTING AI-SPECIFIC CHARACTERISTICS

In Chapter 2 we discussed unique quality characteristics of AI. Let's now look at how to test for some of those characteristics.

### Self-optimising systems

Testing systems that learn from their own experience present several challenges for designing and maintaining tests.

The constraints and behaviour of the system may be clear at the point of release; however, the changes made by a system since that point are not known. The system could have changed in terms of its functional behaviour; these changes may cause previously passing regression tests to fail, even if the changes make the system better overall – another example of a test oracle problem. The system might have found a new way of achieving its goals that may not be easily discovered or analysed.

It is quite important for test design to understand the mechanisms in place to learn for any system. It may be that the system is a shared one used by many stakeholders, not just those at the company implementing it. Using cloud-based AI systems typically constrains the ability for stakeholders to understand or monitor learning, as the details of the process can be hidden from the user.

Even if you are using an internal system and have a great level of control, you might need to think about the timeliness of retraining and test the automation of it. You might also need to consider the resources used; if a system can achieve its goals by using ever more system resources, that might be good for functional behaviour, but eventually cause a failure when those resources run out.

Another non-functional concern is adversarial actors, for example hackers. It might be possible to poison the data or other inputs that the system is learning from in a way that influences its learning and subsequent behaviour.

## Autonomous systems

Purely autonomous systems are those that require no human monitoring or intervention for their operation. However, many such systems have operating parameters that may be breached and trigger them to seek human intervention. It could be necessary to design tests that check how this works and ensure that the system requests intervention (or does not request intervention) in certain scenarios. It is likely to be necessary to manipulate the operating environment significantly in order to check these scenarios.

## Algorithmic, sample and inappropriate bias

Bias is a huge topic that was covered in Chapter 3. Testing for it might include reviewing training and input data (input data testing) or reviewing the methods and decisions in the procurement of those data. It can also include ensuring that the pre-processing of data is being done accurately and without introducing sample bias, and detailed analysis of the outputs of model testing. Further, it can include using explainability tools to understand how particular inputs to the model cause changes in the outputs.

It can sometimes, particularly with inappropriate bias, be very useful to obtain additional data that are not directly processed by the model. This might be demographic or diversity related data, or it might simply be the 'ground truth', that is, a determination of whether the model's predictions were correct.

## NON-DETERMINISTIC SYSTEMS

Non-deterministic systems are those that may produce different outputs each time they are used, even with the same initial state and inputs. Typically, when we execute regression tests on a system, we expect to see the same results as before, whereas with a non-deterministic system we may have multiple valid outputs.

Usually, the solution to this is a deeper understanding of the system in order to define implicit or explicit tolerances that the outputs should meet. It might also be necessary to run them a lot of times, in order to obtain a statistically significant output.

## TRANSPARENCY, EXPLAINABILITY AND INTERPRETABILITY

Transparency and explainability were covered in Chapter 2 and are very important characteristics. Not only do they affect the investigation and resolution of defects, but they are necessary for continuous improvement. Methods and tools for explainability are a rapidly evolving area, but SHAP (Shapley Additive exPlanations) or LIME (Local Interpretable Model-agnostic Explanations) analysis might be a good place to start. These tools allow analysis of how inputs affect outputs and can reveal some odd issues.

For example, in classifying something based on natural language inputs, SHAP analysis might reveal that quite irrelevant words have an excessive influence on the classification.

Sometimes, obtaining an explanation for an action might be something that the user can do themselves through system functionality. Sometimes, there might be a need for an operator to do the same. An important factor here is how easy that is, how timely and how understandable. These aspects fall under 'interpretability', and testing might be performed with the users or operators of the system.

## SUMMARY

In this chapter we have explored how to test ML systems. This is a rapidly evolving field, and it is not yet standardised with clear best practices. It is also worth remembering that there are other types of AI systems, such as reasoning systems, that are not ML and that we haven't covered in this chapter.

# 5 AI-BASED TEST AUTOMATION

## Jeremias Rößler

AI can and has been used in test automation for various tasks and activities. These range from self-healing and self-adaption of automated tests to test generation and test data generation as well as other aspects in between. Test generation and test data generation can happen on all levels, from code level white-box testing (e.g. unit tests) to interface level, to user interface (UI) level. Interestingly enough, test code is the easiest code one can generate. At the same time, sufficiently high code coverage is the enabler through which automated bug fixes and automated code generation is possible. In this chapter I will take you on a journey through all the testing tasks that AI can and is being used for, and will then focus on test generation and test data generation, concluding with an outlook on how code generation will depend on this and can even be the next logical step from here.

The topic 'AI quality' is ambiguous. It can point to the quality of an AI system, but it can also indicate 'AI' as some sort of quality badge – of a system or product that is either produced or has its quality assured by an AI system. In this chapter, we want to explore the latter: a system, that is, software, that has its quality assured by an AI system.

## QUALITY ASSURANCE

Quality assurance is ultimately the domain of humans. In many situations it is difficult to define the desired outcome in an airtight way, considering all possibilities in which that definition can be misinterpreted. That is especially true for software, where many of the 'natural' constraints of the physical world do not apply.

In the digital realm, virtually anything is possible. It is therefore vital to have humans perform the final quality assurance check as to whether the end result meets the defined criteria in an acceptable way, or whether some implicit and unexpressed requirement has been violated. As discussed before, this is called the oracle problem.

### The oracle problem

The oracle problem is the problem of telling right from wrong: whether the outcome of a calculation or process is flawed in any way. The oracle problem applies to individual features of software as much as it applies to the overall software itself: is the outcome of the software development process (i.e. the software) flawed in any way?

In the end it all boils down to context, intent and communication. Whether $12 + 1 = 1$ is correct or not hinges on whether we are in the context of a regular mathematical calculation, or in the context of a date manipulation, calculating a month of a year. For every such decision, there is usually a bigger context to consider, and an intent that has been communicated for that context. Just telling someone you want a photo sharing app could result in the creation of either Snapchat or Instagram, both of which serve that purpose in very different ways.

In real-world software development, it is often the case that the product owner defines the general idea in varying degrees, and the testers and developers fill the remaining gaps by applying common sense. To apply AI to either of these tasks of testing and developing is currently not possible, as the level of common sense needed to fill gaps, infer context and interpret intent would require roughly a human-level of intelligence. Given the comparable efforts and incurred costs of the two tasks, it stands to assume that, if ever AI became powerful enough to achieve either, it would be used to generate the code (which, in itself, is a formal specification of the intended behaviour). As indicated above, it is much easier for a human to check whether some implicit and unexpressed requirement has been violated, than to come up with an original coded solution.

To really understand how hard it is to solve the oracle problem in a general way, one should consider why it is called the 'oracle' problem in the first place: all problems and their respective solutions can be expressed as software, even such outlandish tasks as determining the future or determining whether God exists. Mind you, I am not talking about correct implementations of the solutions to these problems as software, merely about any solution at all. The minimalist implementation of the simplest solution would, for every posed question, always answer with 'yes'. To determine the correctness of that answer to many questions and thus of the software, you would, for example, need to know the future or whether God exists. This is exactly why you would need an oracle from ancient Greek mythology – hence the name.

## TESTING VERSUS TEST AUTOMATION

Software is usually developed in an iterative and incremental way: starting from a first working version, the software is enhanced and improved as version numbers increase. For non-software developers it is often difficult to comprehend how sometimes dependencies connect otherwise unrelated parts of the software in unknown, almost mystical, ways. This means even small changes can have unexpected side effects in unforeseen places. To address this issue, the software has to be continually tested – even parts and features that have already been tested in the past. This essentially requires a lot of repetitive and redundant work, begging for automation. Automation brings the added benefit of speeding up the testing process, allowing testing to be performed ideally after every change.

Note that in the context of this chapter, I am talking about test automation for regression testing or maintenance testing, ignoring other test automation purposes.

However, as the realisation of testing changes with automation, so does its goal. The goal of testing is to find flaws and defects. While this is still technically true for test automation, as per the oracle problem, it cannot be achieved in a general way. Also, it is mostly not necessary: as manual testing has presumably determined the correctness of the software, the goal of test automation changes to ensuring that the software is **still** correct. This means that test automation aims to find unintended and unwanted ways in which the behaviour of the software **changes**.

This is called the consistency oracle: the software should be consistent to former versions of the same software. This oracle can be explicitly defined, as is currently the case in most situations. What is interesting about this, is that the oracle can also be derived: having a previous version of the software for comparison, one can simply execute both versions in parallel and compare the execution results and characteristics. Alternatively, one can store said results and characteristics of the previous version as a baseline and compare against that.

For the consistency oracle to be applicable, it is necessary for the software to be (mostly) deterministic. Also it is very useful to only make small changes to the software and continually compare the changes in behaviour to the baseline and update the baseline with intended changes. Otherwise, one runs the risk of being overwhelmed with too many changes, generating a lot of effort and defying the purpose of the approach.

Since test automation is a huge cost factor and major cause of additional effort and risks, it is a very worthwhile goal for AI to address this problem. In the following section we will focus on this specific task, before addressing other things AI can do in the realm of testing and quality assurance.

## AI IN UNIT TEST AUTOMATION

AI can be used to generate automated tests; however, the level on which this is done dramatically changes the challenges being faced when doing so. In this chapter we will focus specifically on what is often called the code, module, component or unit level.

For many people, this is the desired place to put most of the test automation. This desire is often characterised as the 'test pyramid' (Cohn, 2009) (Figure 5.1).

---

**Figure 5.1 Schematic illustration of the test pyramid** (Source: Based on Cohn, 2009)

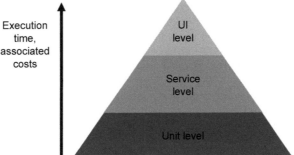

The principal idea is that test automation on the UI level results in brittle tests, where a single small UI change can often result in the inability to correctly execute many of these tests. This often also results in high maintenance costs to fix the tests or high development costs to avoid the problem – or both. Executing these tests usually requires starting the complete system, often multiple times, making it time-consuming to do. On top of that, these tests require a complex software stack with many external dependencies, making them often non-deterministic to run (referred to as 'flakiness'). This non-determinism then results in a lot of false positives, which together with their vulnerability to changes undermines trust and can eventually render UI tests more of a burden than an aid in many projects.

For all these reasons, it is preferable to have the majority of tests at the unit test level. However, these tests do not represent the way the software is consumed and experienced by the end-user, so they are only part of an overall mix of different kinds of tests. It is important to keep that in mind, or else the focus might shift to a purely functional one, disregarding softer aspects like visuals and user experience.

Since these tests reside in the code and are defined in code, they need to be created by developers. An AI system being able to generate these tests would be a huge step towards decreasing their cost. For this reason, a lot of effort has been put into research on how AI could generate these tests. Unfortunately, many challenges still need to be solved to have a market-ready solution. In the following section, we will analyse the different challenges individually.

## Test oracles for unit tests

As has already been established, generating test automation can make use of the consistency oracle. The consistency oracle assumes that the software should be consistent to former versions of the same software. However, while this is true for the software behaviour from a user's perspective, it can be vastly different in regard to the low-level implementation details of that behaviour. This means there needs to be a lot of emphasis on the way the consistency oracle is specified, which in the realm of unit test automation usually happens in the form of assertions. To be robust and non-redundant, an ideal unit test ensures a **single aspect** of the individual **unit under test** – and nothing else. However, from the code level most of the inner state of the system is available or reachable, making it hard for an AI to focus on the current unit under test or the specific aspects currently being ensured. Often, AI ends up ensuring aspects that are non-meaningful or non-relevant. This becomes especially clear if state changes are the desired outcome of an operation. For this reason, much of the academic literature focuses on stateless and side-effect-free operations, such as transformations and calculations.

To illustrate the issues, imagine we want to generate tests for our software. Among the code is an operation `user.setActive()`, where the desired outcome is that the status of the user is changed to 'active'. To detect whether the operation was successful, it is usually not desirable to directly access the inner state of the user – as the AI doesn't know what is relevant, it might decide to assert a specific randomly generated and non-deterministic ID or timestamp. A human-created test would most likely query the user object using its appropriate methods, such as `user.getState()`. Since the user-persistence unit will most likely offer many other operations, deciding to use that specific query operation from all the options is challenging. Of course, these simple examples can be solved by executing the operation multiple times to detect changing aspects. However, in general, deciding which specific aspects of the data should be ensured literally and which in a more abstract manner is hard and determines both the flakiness and the robustness to change of the tests.

Another oracle that is often used on the UI level is the implicit robustness oracle: the software should never crash, no matter what the user does. On the code level, exceptions and crashes may be non-problematic as robustness typically is only ensured on interfaces. So, if the unit under test passes invalid data, such as a null reference, throwing an exception and crashing might be the expected behaviour, rendering this oracle invalid for test generation on the code level.

## Preconditions and parameters

The preconditions necessary to trigger interesting or relevant functionality for a specific unit can be arbitrarily complex. For example, the code might expect an established database connection to exist, that specific environment variables are defined, and so on. Recent advancements in mocking technology (e.g. Mockito) combined with execution path analysis alleviated this problem somewhat; however, similar to the aforementioned challenge of deciding which changes are relevant to a specific unit or aspect being tested, it remains a challenge to automatically decide which behaviour is relevant. If mocking too much, the automated test eventually tests the mock instead of the relevant functionality. If mocking not enough, irrelevant prerequisites are being set up, lowering robustness and making it hard for developers to debug the test, once it fails – essentially turning the test into an integration test.

To illustrate the issues, let us come back to our test for a `save(User)` operation of a user-persistence unit. Establishing a connection to a remote database is somewhat costly and the goal is not to test the internals of the database, which can be safely assumed to work correctly. Therefore, it would make perfect sense to mock the database and just test the persistence logic, for example, the object validation and the correct creation and issuing of the SQL statement. While it is usually a good idea to mock an interface, the challenge is to decide which interface to mock. This could be accomplished, for example, on the communication level of the remote connection, or the API level of the underlying communication framework. Both have the drawback that they merely 'freeze' the current state of the implementation, without verifying its correctness. A change to the underlying SQL schema could cause the unit under test to malfunction or utterly fail in production – but would not be detected by this test. A manually created test on the other hand would probably opt to use an in-memory database instead. Such a database works similarly to an API in that it requires no remote connections, but instead of verifying that the SQL statement is unchanged, it would verify that the SQL statement works for the current schema, even if the latter is subject to change.

Many operations are also being called with complex parameters. In a generated test, these parameters need to be created in a way that matches the intent of the current aspect being tested. Since the aforementioned necessary preconditions can be turned into parameters and vice versa, whether one differentiates this challenge merely depends on the way the code is organised. Often, when talking about complex parameters, the emphasis is on the data and their validity and structure.

To illustrate this, our `save(User)` operation of a user-persistence unit may require a valid email address to be set within the given complex `User` object. It is entirely possible to have the validity of the email address being validated on the database level. Since this code is then outside the scope of the test system and probably not accessible for further analysis during execution, it will be very hard for the test generation system to 'understand' the problem and come up with a valid email address on its own. In this simple scenario, the problem can be easily mitigated if successful and correct executions can be observed and learned from (heeding privacy concerns). However, there are many complex real-world scenarios with intricate dependencies that will be hard for the test generation system to 'understand' and navigate.

## Protocols and internal state

In many real-world scenarios, the unit under test has an internal state that is affected and manipulated by the order in which the related operations (in the following referred to as **methods**) are being called and with which parameters. It is often desirable to verify that this state change is correctly triggered and executed, following a specific (often implicit) protocol. Think about establishing and terminating connections, opening and closing files, and so on. However, deciding whether the change of an internal state is significant or not is a very hard problem, essentially boiling down to the separation of information from noise. The overall number of options multiply per permutation, meaning that with an internal state of 10 Boolean variables, the unit can have $2^{10} =$ 1024 internal states. So, for many real-world systems the number of possible states is already quite large, just considering meaningful differentiations. Without the ability to abstract, the state space of a system can be unfathomably large, or even infinite. This is the reason this challenge has famously been coined the 'state space explosion problem' (E. M. Clarke et al., 2012). This makes it practically impossible to generate tests for every possible state change. So, the test generation system must decide or prioritise what constitutes relevant states and which state changes are relevant to generate tests for.

Let us again illustrate, using our previous user-persistence unit. In order to persist and load `User` objects, the unit will connect to a database in some form. When analysing the internal state of the persistence unit, one must decide about the level of abstraction. This could either mean to treat the connection object as binary (i.e. as existing within the unit or not), or to extend the analysis into the connection object itself. Treating the connection as binary would be too coarse and miss some important cases: for example, the connection object as such could exist, but the underlying network connection may not yet have been established or has been closed already. However, extending the analysis into the connection object would require the same decision regarding abstraction recursively at each level. Every data point tracked is a potential differentiator for internal state. Is the exact timestamp relevant? The difference to the current time? If so, in which granularity? This is already hard for humans to understand, or else we wouldn't need to test in the first place. And eventually the decision about which abstractions make sense boils down to be an instance of the famous halting-problem: the only surefire way for all possible programs to know whether a specific change in state makes a difference or whether it can be abstracted away, is to **execute** the program.

## Test code generation

The result of unit test generation is usually unit tests in the form of code. Most developers think that the structure and readability of code is very important, provoking trends and movements, such as the software craftmanship manifesto (Manifesto for Software Craftsmanship, n.d.) and the clean code initiative (Clean Code Developer, n.d.), and static analysis tools that check for 'code smells'.[1] This attitude is understandable, given that code is read 10 times as often as it is written (Martin, 2008). However, 'readability' is more of an art than an easy and straightforward concept, making it difficult to put it into hard rules. This is further complicated by the fact that each language and often each test framework have different concepts of how readable code looks.

## Clear focus and intent

This has an overlap with some other challenges. As has been discussed, an ideal unit test ensures a **single aspect** of the individual **unit under test** – and nothing else. A human ideally would analyse a specific unit or feature and define both the intended use cases and some probable edge cases, and then create a test for each of these. Test-driven development actually proposes to create these tests before the actual implementation. This is a top-down approach.

Lacking the understanding and context, a test generation system will instead typically apply a bottom-up approach: analyse the code and its behaviour and then generate tests for each specific case, trying to cover as much code as possible. Both approaches have their benefits and drawbacks: while a top-down approach is somewhat more structured and allows for a 'logical' differentiation of the test cases, a bottom-up approach can detect specific cases that, according to specification, should not even exist, but somehow got implemented. This is an instance of the oracle problem: deciding whether an existing case of specific and distinct behaviour is intended or constitutes an error.

Obviously, the challenge of focus and intent is very closely related to the question of protocols and internal state: what constitutes relevant states and which state changes are relevant to generate tests for. However, an additional aspect that hasn't been discussed so far is the problem of the overall prioritisation: when is a specific function, unit or aspect tested 'enough' in comparison to the rest of the system?

## AI in unit testing: summary

As can be seen, there are challenges when trying to generate tests on the unit level. However, due to the expected gains in efficiency, it is still an area of ongoing research, resulting in both commercial tools and free-to-use open-source tools. One open-source tool that generates unit tests for existing code is EvoSuite (Fraser, n.d.).

## AI IN UI LEVEL TEST AUTOMATION

Many of the challenges that arise when generating tests on the unit level are much smaller or do not arise at all when generating tests on the UI level or the system level (Gross et al., 2012).

---

1   A code smell is considered a bad coding practice in most situations, but since there are legitimate exceptions, there are no hard rules.

## Test oracles for UI tests

While both the consistency oracle and the implicit robustness oracle do not apply easily or at all at the unit or code level, they both **do** apply on the user interface level. The user values consistency from one version to another, so it is vital to change the user interface carefully and deliberately. Any unintended side effect and non-approved change **is** a defect. Thus, the consistency oracle can be used to verify the consistency of the system boundary over iterations of the software. Differences on that boundary between versions of the software tend to be meaningful and, in any case, have a much lower noise ratio – if the software is deterministic.

The robustness oracle applies as well: from a user perspective, the software must not crash ever, no matter the input. Therefore, any crash that can be triggered **is** a defect. Also, the software should respond within a certain amount of time.

Interestingly enough, all of the above observations hold true for any system interface, even for technical ones, including APIs.

## Preconditions, parameters, repeatability and interdependence

For the UI to be available, usually the complete system must be started. For most self-contained software, this creates all the necessary preconditions by itself (i.e. it loads the configuration, establishes the database connection, and so on), solving the aforementioned challenge that arises for unit tests.

However, the fact that the complete software must be started (or at least reset) each time a test executes well adds to the problem of the long-running execution cycles of these kinds of tests, as was mentioned earlier. Also, the side effects of executing certain tests tend to be long-lasting, whether it's the creation, alteration or deletion of data, or the change of configuration. This often results in tests being interdependent, as they access the same data or configuration. Worse still, this interdependence is often created involuntarily and thus exists secretly, only exposed by one or several problems arising over time.

Tests being interdependent is highly undesirable for a variety of reasons. As has just been explained, UI tests tend to have long execution cycles. An easy remedy is parallelisation and prioritisation, both of which are unavailable to interdependent tests. Interdependence also routinely results in brittleness of already fragile tests, increasing complexity of cause–effect analysis and associated costs of maintenance (when both software **and** tests change). The easiest such case, but fortunately also the most common one, is that if one test fails, it will result in a couple of dependent tests failing as well, obfuscating the original cause. The analysis is much more difficult if tests depend on one another in more subtle ways, such as one test changing some data, maybe even involuntarily or implicitly, that another test depends on. This also makes manual debugging much more difficult, resulting in 'Heisenberg Bugs' (or 'Heisenbugs'), that is, problems that vanish once someone tries to debug them.

Another challenge that was discussed, is the generation of input parameters. On the code level, literally anything can be turned into an input parameter: from complex data objects to database connections. On the other hand, when generating tests for the UI, input parameters consist only of primitives, such as point and click operations and strings as being generated mostly for individual input fields. Complex input data (such as valid XML) are very rarely needed (obviously depending on the type of UI under test). This often allows for either a brute-force generation of the necessary data, or for individual recordings to be reused. This is further facilitated, in that existing protocols tend to be enforced or at least hinted at by the UI design.

## Monkey testing

Have you ever marvelled at how vast infinity is? It is unfathomable. And one of the many fascinating facts is that a truly random series of numbers (i.e. one that never repeats itself, ever) contains all the other numbers. This means that the Archimedes' constant $\pi$ does contain the bible – and every edition and every language thereof.

Following this reasoning, the infinite monkey theorem states that a monkey randomly hitting keys on a typewriter for an infinite amount of time will eventually type any text, including the complete works of William Shakespeare. The term 'monkey testing' is derived from both this theorem and the, often nonsensical, way of interacting with the system. It should be noted that, according to the monkey theorem, monkey testing already completely solves the problem of generating every possible test for the system, given enough time. The only remaining problem is that 'infinity' is an impractical amount of time, for most projects anyway. So, adding heuristics and AI to the monkey is meant to make it more efficient, that is, the monkey gets to more meaningful tests faster.

Monkey testing is just a means to generate test executions, but these then obviously lack the test oracles. Thus, they are traditionally only used in conjunction with the implicit test oracle that a system should not crash no matter what the user does. With that intent, monkey testing has been used since the 1980s, to test systems for robustness and stability.

Fuzz testing is the use of a (pseudo) random number generator to produce test data. In a sense, user interaction – clicking, swiping, as well as text input – can be considered as a special kind of randomly generated test data. Therefore, monkey testing is a special case of fuzz testing, but restricted in the type of data generated and the type of interface applicable.

This means that for monkey testing, similar AI approaches can be applied as for fuzz testing: genetic algorithms can be used to generate variations and combinations of existing (recorded) test cases. Neural networks can also be used and trained on what a typical user would do (i.e. which fields and buttons would be used and in what order). This is essentially comparing graphical user interface (GUI) usage to playing a game: in any given GUI state, the AI must decide what move to make next (i.e. what user interaction to perform). Most interesting is that the knowledge that becomes encoded in such neural networks is often not tied to any particular software – part of it represents general rules for user experience design, such as Fitts' law.[2]

---

2  Fitts' law predicts the time a human needs for a specific movement, such as pointing a mouse before clicking, depending on the distance and size of the target.

These approaches can even be combined. An evolutionary algorithm starts with a seed population. This seed population can either be generated by humans (e.g. recordings of user stories or user interactions), or it can be randomly generated. The better the seed population, the better and faster the results. So, if the seed population is (partially) randomly generated, a neural network can be used to generate more human-like tests.

In contrast to playing a game, where the goal for the AI (to win) is clear, the goal in testing is not so clear. The goal must be measurable by the AI in a fully automated way, so manually evaluated 'soft' criteria are not usable. A naïve goal would be maximal code coverage, but that often results in tests that are unrealistic or non-sensible from a user perspective. A more sensible goal would be input coverage or coverage of controls. Choosing the right goal has a strong effect on how the AI algorithm performs.

## Test selection and prioritisation

As has been detailed before, UI tests tend to be long-running tests. This can quickly result in a situation where there are simply too many automated tests to run regularly, as best practice would have it, such as per commit, per pull request or even per night. Even with parallelisation, the required computational power and the associated costs can be excessive compared with the perceived benefits. And on top of that, brittleness and fragility result in many failing tests, each of which needs to be examined and can often turn out to be a false positive. All of these are strong arguments for test selection and prioritisation.

Test prioritisation utilises runtime information, such as code coverage and test similarity of execution paths, and can be further enhanced by historical information, such as test effectiveness, that is, number and criticality of defects discovered in the past (Juergens et al., 2011).

## Object identification and identifier selection

Object identification is a challenge that is unique to UI testing and does not occur in other testing scenarios, but, for example, in robotic process automation (RPA). The test system must interact with the software under test, both to simulate the user input and to verify expected results. This requires the same UI elements, such as buttons, text fields and labels, to be reliably re-identified. If this is not possible anymore, the test fails, often representing a false positive.

The most crude and fragile method for doing so, but sometimes also the last resort, is using X/Y coordinates. Obviously, this not only breaks with any changes in resolution and layout, it is also hard to maintain without any comments as to which object was intended in the first place. It can even lead to some hard-to-identify situations, where the text was entered into the wrong field, or the wrong button was clicked. A somewhat better method is using XPath or similar (the internal unique path of the element within the GUI), although this can also be subject to change. Obviously preferable are semantic identification criteria, such as ID or name, but even these can change.

AI can help to identify the correct object based on a variety of identification criteria (e.g. XPath, label, ID, class, X/Y coordinates), based on the 'look' of the object by applying some form of image recognition, or by selecting the most historically stable single identification criterion. All these approaches have been used in the past.

### Visual test automation

Visual test automation addresses the specific problem that sometimes software is technically correct in the information that is being shown, but becomes practically unusable or 'ugly'. It aims exclusively to identify visual differences on different platforms (cross-platform and cross-device testing) or visual regressions. This includes unintended changes in a GUI's position, size, layout, font, colour or other visible attributes; whether some objects are difficult to see or outright inaccessible; or visual artefacts or other issues. Visual test automation does not aim to test functional or business aspects of the software.

### AI in UI level test automation: summary

By now it should have become obvious that testing software on the UI level is much easier than testing it on the code level – although many challenges remain to be solved. One of the main advantages is probably that no coding skills are required at this level, making the technology accessible to a much wider audience.

## APPLYING AI TO OTHER TASKS IN SOFTWARE QUALITY ASSURANCE

In order to manage and assure the quality of a piece of software, there are many more tasks required than merely testing the software. However, the range of tasks is so wide, and the number of possibilities of how AI can support it so vast, that it is prohibitive to provide a near-complete list. Instead, we will name the most likely candidates of tasks that will be supported by AI in the foreseeable future.

Note that some of the tasks (such as test data generation, test optimisation or test selection) are needed for the already discussed generation of tests, and therefore have also been discussed above.

### Bug triaging

For large projects with hundreds of thousands of users or more, a considerable amount of effort goes into the management of bug reports – especially if there are automated bug reporting systems (e.g. for Microsoft Windows, Firefox or similar). Up to a fourth of bug reports can be duplicates. Clustering algorithms can be used to remove duplicates and point out particularly critical bugs that are responsible for a large percentage of bug reports (Bettenburg et al., 2008).

### Anomaly detection

Anomaly detection is something that comes quite 'naturally' to AI and can be used in a variety of use cases. This includes, for instance, live monitoring of production systems or test systems, looking for incidences or 'strange behaviour' that can show human or system faults or even security breaches. Things that can be monitored include network traffic, input/output behaviour, log messages, API call usage, disk space, central processing unit and memory consumption and many more.

## Risk prediction and fault estimation

The analysis of change patterns in software repositories and comparison with historical data about bug occurrences has so far only been applied in scientific research. Correlating these data with yet unreleased changes allows us to make predictions about the riskiness of these changes and the likeliness that they will introduce new bugs or cause post-release problems (Zimmermann et al., 2009).

It should be noted that this approach suffers from the pesticide paradox in that the effectiveness decreases over time, just as pesticides fail to kill insects after a certain period of usage.

## Effort estimation for manual testing

The analysis of change patterns in software repositories mentioned above also allows us to point out the most problematic changes and have a more targeted manual testing and review process. This in turn lets managers somewhat adjust the efforts for testing – that is, low-risk releases need less testing.

## Defect analysis

This is a task that often needs to happen fast and usually takes a lot of effort. Additional to that, it ties into several interesting research topics, such as test generation, code analysis, execution analysis and automated programming. This topic is therefore constantly being researched and a lot of interesting approaches have been developed – however, none is available for purchase at the time of writing. One of the more interesting applications is the SapFix system, which even automatically generates fixes for technical errors (Jia et al., 2018).

Defects can be analysed from a lot of different angles, resulting in various ways that manual analysis can be sped up or, for example, tickets assigned to the ideal development resource. This includes the generation of additional tests for cause–effect chain analysis, stack trace analysis, execution path analysis and more.

## Applying AI to other tasks: summary

These brief examples show the wide variety of ways AI can be used to support humans in development and quality assurance. We remain curious as to what unexpected approaches the future holds for us.

## EVALUATING TOOL SUPPORT FOR TESTING

It is rarely useful to implement any of the aforementioned techniques directly in a typical project context. Instead, a tool vendor or platform provider would provide a tool that you then can choose to use. Therefore, this section will be the most applicable for most projects: how do you decide whether any given approach should be used and how do you choose between multiple available tools implementing an approach?

## Metrics for an AI-based testing approach

In principle, an AI-based quality assurance tool is both an AI system like any other, and a quality assurance tool like any other – so the same metrics can be applied.

One of the requirements of a task that is given to AI-based systems, to counter the no-free-lunch theorem,[3] is that the past is a good predictor of the future. However, 'good' is a somewhat fuzzy concept in many real-world scenarios. For example, in 'Risk prediction and fault estimation', one must be aware of both the pesticide paradox and the effect of self-fulfilling prophecies, which ironically have opposite effects: focusing testing effort on certain parts of the system will initially result in more errors and higher risk being indicated because the system will be tested more intensively at those points (self-fulfilling prophecy). After some time, as the quality of the code and the awareness of developers and manual testers increases, the pesticide paradox will kick in and the effectiveness of the prediction will decrease.

Typical metrics for AI-based approaches include the false positives (type I errors) and false negatives (type II errors). However, for many real-world problems, the latter are hard to measure. For instance, the type II errors of missed bugs in a system are often impossible to determine (i.e. it is hard to know how many bugs were not detected). Another aspect to consider is the severity of the defects that are found by the test cases, even if they cause a crash. It is not unlikely that the tool finds defects that in principle have a high severity (because they cause a crash), but no customer would ever use the software in the way necessary to trigger the defects. Reporting such defects may even have a negative net effect by diverting focus from more customer-relevant tasks or by spamming the ticket system. Therefore, it is not the number of bugs that is important, but the associated risk or impact on customers, which is even harder to measure.

However, unusual behaviours are often how adversarial agents attempt to access a system. So if the testing goal is security testing, then vulnerabilities, even obscure ones, are important to find.

## Assessing claims of tool vendors

Many tool vendors have perfected their marketing to provide a most compelling story. And since AI became en vogue, this story often contains some sort of AI. However, one should not buy a tool for the tool's sake and AI for AI's sake, so, it does not really matter whether AI is part of a solution – which it often even isn't. According to a 2019 report by MMC on some 2,830 AI start-ups in 13 EU countries, they could find no evidence of AI in 40 per cent of cases (MMC, 2019). It is reasonable to assume that when describing software products, such as testing tools, a similar amount of leeway is used in defining 'AI'.

A healthy dose of scepticism should be applied when reviewing vendor claims. Whether AI is actually part of a proper solution is more of an academic question, as long as the

---

3   The no-free-lunch theorem states that any two optimisation algorithms (including completely random ones) are equivalent when their performance is averaged across all possible problems. In order for any approaches (such as AI) to be superior, specific assumptions in regards to the problems have to be made – such as that the past is a good predictor of the future.

tool performs as promised by the vendor. However, the performance is exactly what should be critically examined. Management's expectations of an AI-based testing tool can also differ and even be unrealistic, putting the tool's proponents in a difficult position if the tool fails to meet these expectations. In general, many tools work quite well for small examples, but scale poorly for larger projects, so make sure to account for that when performing the evaluation.

Unfortunately, many projects run into a chicken-and-egg problem: in order to realistically evaluate a tool, it has to be set up and configured (or even trained) properly. So, most of the effort must be invested before anything can even be evaluated. This in turn means one needs to resort to looking at the vendor's previous implementations of the product and ideally talk to existing or past customers.

## Return on investment

Ultimately, management typically will want to see some sort of ROI calculation. This can be hard to do for several reasons:

(i) Depending on the processes in place, some of the metrics are easier to get and are more objective, such as number of bugs, number of customer requests or downtime. Depending on the accuracy of the tracking tools, one can derive metrics like effort in hours per bug and, based on that, costs per bug. However, most of the intuitive metrics are the wrong type of metrics (as opposed to merely being irrelevant) and don't account for things like customer sentiments or lost sales due to, for example, bad ratings.

(ii) Depending on the selected metrics, expected reductions are hard to extrapolate – even with such seemingly objective measures as number of bugs. However, it is even more complicated, as the results range from effects that are subtle or unobtrusive, all the way to completely redesigning processes by adding capabilities. In some situations, the added value diminishes over time, making it even more difficult to estimate.

(iii) There will also probably be additional and unforeseen costs. These come from needing special knowledge and experience, effort for maintaining the system or reviewing findings (e.g. manually going through a lot of false positives regularly). Ironically enough, a tool can also introduce additional risk (e.g. false negatives).

In order to get at least a rough estimate of the potential costs and savings, it is sensible to consider several questions: what impact will this system have on existing processes? For example, will you need to recreate or migrate artefacts such as existing automated tests? Will it integrate well with existing infrastructure, such as your existing test and reporting systems, continuous integration/continuous deployment (CI/CD) systems, release systems, documentation systems or ticket systems? Will it cause employees to change their behaviour (e.g. blind trust in the system through complacency or automation)? Will employees need additional training? Could there be unintended long-term effects?

## Assessing test case generation tools

In the case of test case generation tools, there are several specific considerations and questions to be asked: are the generated tests realistic in that they represent typical or sensible usage? Do they cover key business risks, that is, do the generated test cases cover relevant user scenarios? Are the data used (or generated) representative of typical data? Is it even possible for the AI to generate realistic test cases without additional training? If not, how is such training possible, that is, what is the input to the AI system in terms of training data? Is it sufficient to merely record test cases?

When adding test cases to a project, the added value per test case decreases with the number of test cases added. The first test case is much more valuable than the thousandth. More test cases come with higher maintenance costs, slower execution cycles, higher life cycle management complexity and many other hidden costs. These costs should be outweighed by the benefits that the added test cases bring, so it is important to determine what the marginal costs are. Generated test cases are usually difficult for humans to understand (e.g. determining the goal of a particular test case) and therefore difficult to maintain. Sometimes a small detail makes a test valuable (e.g. in terms of coverage by checking a particular option). If the maintainer does not know what makes the test valuable in comparison to the others when maintaining it, a valuable test can easily be turned into useless ballast. All things considered, generated test cases are often cheap to generate, but expensive to maintain. What are the criteria for discarding the generated test cases and simply starting from scratch?

### Evaluation tool support: summary

It has been shown that many questions have to be asked and answered in order to evaluate tool support in quality assurance – whether AI based or not. Unfortunately, the right answers for many of the questions are situation- and project-specific, closing the loop all the way back to the oracle problem, that is, determining what actually constitutes 'correct'. Therefore, the goal of this chapter was to give an idea of what aspects to look at and what to consider when evaluating tools. We hope this will be of much more long-term value than giving concrete answers, which will be short-lived and ultimately wrong for most situations anyway.

## TASKS THAT WILL LIKELY REMAIN CHALLENGING FOR AI

There are some tasks in the realm of quality assurance that will likely remain challenging for AI. These include gathering and challenging specifications and assumptions, communication with stakeholders, improving processes and organisations and many more. Should there be significant improvements in that regard, the chances are that these will have a more significant impact in other fields (such as management in general), so that the effects on quality assurance will pale in comparison.

As was discussed at the beginning of this chapter, the specification of test oracles, that is, the final assessment of the result of the software design and development process, will most likely remain a manual task – even if all else gets automated. This will entail communication with stakeholders to clarify ambiguities and retrieve missing information. Like the development of autonomous cars, we should not expect sudden leaps in AI in the field of quality assurance, but instead a steady improvement in the way these tools assist us with our daily chores.

## SUMMARY

AI can be used in very different ways when being applied to quality assurance. In this chapter, we have shown applications to the unit, interface and user interface levels, all of which come with their own respective challenges and solutions. And as technology progresses, many more yet unforeseen approaches are to be expected.

However, it is rarely the duty of testing practitioners to envision or develop such tools – so the intention of the last part of this chapter was to provide the knowledge necessary for the far more likely duty: to evaluate and decide on a tool and then apply it in practice.

Many testing experts are afraid of using AI, fearing that it will threaten their jobs in the long term. From our point of view, it should be consoling that AI will much more likely replace software developers (at least partially) than it will replace software testers. With Microsoft Copilot and OpenAI Codex, the first big steps in that direction have already been taken and many more will surely follow.

# 6 ONTOLOGIES FOR SOFTWARE TESTING

## Joanna Isabelle Olszewska

In AI, ontologies describe a formal specification of a certain domain, that is, a shared understanding of a domain of interest as well as a formal and machine-understandable model of this domain. Hence, ontologies can be used for capturing, sharing, and representing software testing knowledge in a systematic and interoperable way. Furthermore, ontologies support automated reasoning about that knowledge to assist **intelligent agents (IAs)**, whether human beings or artificial systems, in their task of testing software and systems.

## ABOUT ONTOLOGIES

Ontologies appeared in philosophy and focused on the study of the 'subject of existence'. In information technology (IT), they are often seen as taxonomies or hierarchies of classes, but ontologies are much more than that.

Let's take a closer look at their use in computer science, encompassing artificial intelligence, software engineering, and especially software testing.

### Ontologies in computer science

Three decades ago, ontologies started to be studied in computer science and became a pillar of the semantic web, which perceives an ontology as a body of formally represented knowledge based on a conceptualisation.

In computer science, an ontology aims to represent concepts with all their interdependent properties. Hence, classes and their instances (also called individuals) can be populated within the ontology and related through their defined properties.

> An ontology is 'an explicit specification of a conceptualization' (Gruber, 1995).

Ontologies have been developed for a wide range of computing applications, such as programming-by-example (Gordon et al., 2010), cloud computing (Al Feel and Khafagy, 2011) and cybersecurity (Simmons et al., 2014), to name a few among more than 137,000 semantic web documents that can be retrieved from the web, for example by Swoogle, the semantic web search engine (Ding et al., 2004).

This popularity of ontologies in computer science has led to the rise of the field called **ontology engineering** (Gomez-Perez et al., 2004), which deals with the ontology development process, ontology life cycle, methods and methodologies, tools, and languages for building ontologies.

In particular, several methodologies to build ontologies have been proposed in the literature. For example, **METHONTOLOGY** (Fernandez et al., 1997) is a mature process to support the development and the integration of ontologies, but does not offer the possibility of reusing existing ontologies at an early stage in the process.

Another example is **Toronto virtual enterprise (TOVE)** (Gruninger and Fox, 1995). This modelling methodology comprehends the complete ontology development life cycle, but is usually too complex for small-scale applications and does not allow the reuse of ontologies either. More specifically, the TOVE approach considers ontological primitives as concepts, relations, and axioms. In addition, TOVE involves, on one hand, the formulation of **competency questions (CQs)** (Wisniewski et al., 2019) that the ontology must be able to answer correctly. Indeed, CQs can be seen as a set of ontology requirements as well as a way of scoping and delimiting the subject domain that has to be represented in the ontology. On the other hand, it implies the axiomatisation (Staab and Maedche, 2000) of the ontology, leading to the identification and definition of **axioms**, since the ontology should contain a necessary and sufficient set of axioms to represent and solve these CQs.

It is worth noting that axioms (Vasilecas et al., 2009) can be of different types and nature. Hence, axioms generally express and restrict complex relationships between concepts and constrain their intended interpretation. In particular, derivation axioms allow new information to be derived from the previously existing knowledge. Epistemological axioms are defined to show constraints imposed by the way concepts are structured, while ontological axioms describe domain signification constraints. Moreover, consolidation axioms typically impose constraints that must be satisfied for a relation to be consistently established.

A further methodology is **enterprise ontology (EO)** (Dietz and Mulder, 2020). This covers the whole ontology development life cycle and allows the sharing of common understanding of the structure of information among people or software agents.

All these methodologies differ in terms of life cycle coverage of the ontological development process or in terms of definitions of the different tasks and stages. However, some general tasks to develop ontologies have been identified (Olszewska, 2015). They mainly consist of knowledge selection, analysis, and description, and they are usually performed during four phases, namely, ontology specification, conceptualisation, implementation, and evaluation.

Furthermore, specific ontological programming languages have been developed by the **World Wide Web Consortium (W3C)** for ontological domain modelling and knowledge representation. For this purpose, the **Resource Description Framework (RDF)** (2021) is a model for data interchange on the web, which is used to create metadata and descriptions, while the **Web Ontology Language (OWL)** (2021) is a semantic web language designed to represent rich and complex knowledge about concepts, groups of concepts, and relations between these concepts. Moreover, OWL is a computational logic-based language such that knowledge expressed in OWL can be exploited by computer programs, for example to verify the consistency of that knowledge or to make implicit knowledge explicit.

Three variants of the OWL standard language exist and are named OWL-Lite, OWL-DL and OWL-Full, respectively. Most of the operational ontologies (Ferreira de Souza et al., 2013) adopt the OWL-DL language, which is the variant of OWL language based on **description logics (DL)** (Baader et al., 2003). It is worth noting that DL combines a rigorous, semantics based-on first-order predicate logic with an intuitive way of structuring and encoding expressive conceptual knowledge. Therefore, OWL-DL offers mathematical formalisation along with more semantic expressiveness than the less-used, simpler variant called OWL-Lite. It is also possible to perform **automated reasoning** on OWL-DL-based ontologies (Olszewska et al., 2014).

**Automated reasoning** is an advanced area of computer science that is concerned with applying reasoning in the form of logic to computing systems, in order to make inferences automatically (Wos et al., 2021).

Automated reasoning aims to produce programs that allow computers to reason automatically. Although the overall goal is to mechanise different forms of reasoning, the term 'automated reasoning' has thus largely been identified with valid deductive reasoning as practised in mathematics and formal logic (Portoraro, 2021).

Hence, OWL-DL enables the use of a reasoner to compute the inferred ontology class hierarchy and to perform internal consistency checks. Moreover, OWL-DL's reasoners are tractable, that is, work in polynomial time, whereas in the case of OWL-Full, which is the variant uniting OWL syntax and RDF data representation, automated reasoning is not tractable. Consequently, OWL-DL's reasoners are computationally more efficient than OWL-Full's ones.

On the other hand, ontologies can also follow a context-adaptive approach (Holzinger et al., 2018), that is, classical logical ontological approaches can be combined with statistical approaches to build stochastic ontologies.

Besides, ontological tools (e.g. ontology-based software development environment (ODE) (de Almeida Falbo et al., 2003), and WebODE (Arpirez et al., 2001)) have been elaborated to help computer scientists in developing ontologies. In particular, a well-established open-source ontology editor is called **Protégé** (Protégé, 2021). It is a stand-alone tool that provides an integrated knowledge-based editing environment with rich graphical menus (Horridge, 2011), which allows conceptualisation, visualisation and manipulation of ontologies. Furthermore, Protégé can generate OWL files that can be accessed from different programming language platforms like **XML** or **Java** (Horridge and Bechhofer, 2011), and/or that can be directly published on the **World Wide Web (www)**. Protégé is also accessible on the cloud through **WebProtégé** for collaborative editing of ontologies.

Both **Protégé** and **WebProtégé** benefit from a live, supporting community that can be reached via Twitter @protegeproject. Moreover, WebProtégé appears to be the most used tool to develop ontologies, as per the following tweet posted on 19 March 2021:

'20 years after @protegeproject is still the most mentioned tool !'

https://twitter.com/i/web/status/1372856305560457225

## Ontologies and artificial intelligence

Nowadays, an ontology is considered as an AI technique that is part of the **knowledge representation (KR)** field and that is constituted by a specific vocabulary used to describe a certain reality, plus a set of explicit assumptions regarding the intended meaning of the vocabulary, in a formal way that AIs can interpret (Noy and McGuinness, 2001).

**Knowledge representation** is the field of AI dedicated to representing information about the world in a form that a computer system can use to solve complex tasks. Knowledge representation incorporates findings from: (i) psychology about how humans solve problems and represent knowledge in order to design formalisms that will make complex systems easier to design and build; and (ii) logic to automate various kinds of reasoning, such as the application of rules or the relations of sets and subsets (Davis et al., 1993).

Knowledge representation thus makes complex software easier to define and maintain than procedural code and can be used in expert systems.

Ontological knowledge representation allows **automated reasoning** on the ontology terms and axioms. For this purpose, an inbuilt reasoner, which is a logic-based inference engine such as HermiT (Glimm et al., 2014) or FaCT++ (Tsarkov, 2014), is run on the ontology, which usually owns a set of axioms called terminological box (TBox) describing classes and properties as a domain vocabulary, and a set of axioms called assertion box (ABox) describing assertions about the individuals based on the terminology. The reasoner is then able to answer both intentional queries (e.g. regarding concept satisfiability) and extensional queries (e.g. retrieving the instances of a given concept).

Ontological knowledge representation also features **interoperability**, which is crucial for AI communication and collaboration. Indeed, interoperability (Uschold and Gruninger, 1996) is the ability of agents to correctly and automatically interpret the intended meaning of concepts within some context or domain and use them properly in their local applications. Ontologies are thus a useful knowledge representation for AI applications ranging from computer vision (Olszewska and McCluskey, 2011) to robotics (Olszewska, 2018a), including intelligent vision systems (IVS) (Olszewska, 2018b), multi-agent systems (MAS) (Berrani et al., 2018), cloud robotics systems (CRS) (Pignaton de Freitas et al., 2020b), and **Industry 4.0 (I4.0)** (Sampath Kumar et al., 2019). Indeed, one major aspect of I4.0 is to adopt a coherent approach for the semantic communication between multiple intelligent systems, which include human and artificial (software or hardware) agents. For this purpose, ontologies can provide the solution by formalising the smart manufacturing knowledge in an interoperable way (Sampath Kumar et al., 2019).

> **Industry 4.0** is a term coined to represent the fourth industrial revolution driven by the latest technological advances, based on digital data, connectivity, cyber systems and AI. It results in smart products, smart machines, and/or augmented operators, but also in challenges such as interoperability (Slee et al., 2021).

Other important properties of ontologies are their **shareability** and **reusability,** which allow available ontological knowledge to be used as input to generate new ontologies (Katsumi and Gruninger, 2016). This is particularly useful when developing large-scale ontologies for complex domains or intelligent systems, such as AI-based systems. Hence, some methodologies to develop ontologies propose to build an ontology by reusing existing ontologies (i.e. by assembling, extending, specialising, and adapting other ontologies that are parts of the resulting ontology) (Pinto, 1999), while some other approaches allow the building of an ontology by merging different ontologies on the same subject into a single one that unifies all of them (Uschold et al., 1998).

It is also worth noting that there are three main types of ontologies (Wu and Hakansson, 2014), as follows. Firstly, a **core ontology** is a basic and minimal ontology consisting only of the minimal concepts required to understand the other concepts. For example, the core ontology for robotics and automation (CORA) (Fiorini et al., 2017), which is described in the IEEE 1872-2015 ontological standard for automation systems and robotics, defines core concepts that form the basis of robotic systems and automation. Secondly, a **domain ontology** intends to represent all/most of the concepts that belong to a realm of the world, for example cloud-robotic-system domain ontology (ROCO) (Pignaton de Freitas et al., 2020a), spatio-temporal, visual domain ontology (STVO) (Olszewska, 2011), or explainable artificial intelligence (XAI) ontology (Seeliger et al., 2019). Thirdly, an **upper ontology**, such as the suggested upper merged ontology (SUMO) (2021), the unified foundational ontology (UFO) (Guizzardi, 2005), or the descriptive ontology for linguistic and cognitive engineering (DOLCE) (2021), is a model of the commonly shared relations and objects that are generally applicable across a wide range of domain ontologies.

Hence, for example, the reuse and the sharing of ontologies enable the ROCO domain ontology for cloud robotics systems to integrate the robotic core ontology (CORA), which in turn is based on the SUMO upper ontology. This also supports the modelling and evaluation of complex systems, such as **smart systems** (Slee et al., 2021) or **systems of systems** (Yan et al., 2014).

> A **System of Systems (SoS)** is a collection of independent systems, integrated into a larger system that delivers unique capabilities. The independent constituent systems collaborate to produce some global behaviour that they cannot produce alone (Boardman and Sauser, 2006).

## Ontologies in context of software engineering

Since ontologies intrinsically allow us to represent knowledge unambiguously, to share information in an interoperable way and to perform automated reasoning, they have been used in the software engineering domain (Pop et al., 2014) by various stakeholders (Murtazinam and Avdeenko, 2018) or multiple agents (Sugawara et al., 2011). Such ontologies have been used for supporting the requirement engineering process (Avdeenko and Pustovalova, 2016), software development (Olszewska and Allison, 2018), software maintenance (Nor et al., 2012), or quality assurance inspections (Da Silva et al., 2015). So, what about ontologies for software testing? Let's examine them.

## USING ONTOLOGIES FOR SOFTWARE TESTING

Software testers have been using dedicated ontologies for software testing for more than a decade (Chen and Xi, 2020).

Indeed, ontologies have been developed for supporting test development (Landhausser and Genaid, 2012) and test automation (Paydar and Kahani, 2010), including test generation (Nasser et al., 2010), test execution (Yu et al., 2009), test management (Sapna and Mohanty, 2011), and test reuse (Lim and Zhang, 2012).

Moreover, ontology-driven software testing has been applied to perform specific tests (Klueck et al., 2018):

- for different software testing practice (e.g. requirement-based testing (Feldmann et al., 2014), behaviour-driven development (BDD) (Rocha Silva et al., 2017));

- for different software testing techniques (e.g. mutation testing) (Wang et al., 2009);

- for different software testing types such as functional testing (e.g. regression testing (Campos et al., 2017), graphical user interface testing (Li et al., 2009)) and non-functional testing (e.g. dependability testing (Looker et al., 2005), performance testing (Freitas and Vieira, 2014), security testing (Siqueira Bueno et al., 2018), or usability testing (Robal et al., 2017));

- for different software applications such as APIs (Alqahtani et al., 2017) and web services (Wang et al., 2007).

However, there are only a few examples of software testing ontologies that present both conceptual and implementation models of the software testing domain. So, let's analyse them in terms of ontology purpose and scope, referenced **body of knowledge (BoK)** and domain coverage as well as developed main ontological concepts.

### Example 1. Software Testing Ontology for Web Service ontology

The first established ontology that has been developed for software testing is called **Software Testing Ontology for Web Service (STOWS)** (Huo et al., 2003). This ontology is a multi-agent integrated software environment for web-based test services and helps to perform the matching between testing tasks and the tester's capability. On one hand, the testing tasks include each testing activity and related information about how the activity is required to be performed, such as the context, the testing method to use, the environment in which the activity is to be carried out, the available resources, and the requirements on the test results. On the other hand, the tester's capability is determined by the activities that a tester can perform together with the context for the agent to perform the activity, the testing method used, the environment to perform the testing, the required resources (i.e. the input), and the output that the tester can generate.

STOWS presents 63 terms around six main concepts, which are:

- tester (e.g. human, software agent, team);
- context (e.g. unit testing, integration testing, system testing);
- activity (e.g. test planning, test case generation, test execution, test result verification, test coverage measurement, test report generation);
- method (e.g. error-based testing, fault-based testing, structural testing);
- artefacts (e.g. intermediate data, testing result, test plans, test suites, test scripts);
- environment (e.g. hardware, software).

Hence, STOWS covers aspects related to testing activities, testing artefacts, testing methods, testing type, testing environment and capability, but is not compliant to any specific referenced BoK, and no ontological methodology has been followed to develop it.

### Example 2. OntoTest ontology

The **OntoTest** (Barbosa et al., 2006) ontology was developed to provide a reference architecture for software engineering tools, in order to support acquisition, organisation, reuse, and sharing of testing knowledge. It is based on the ISO/IEC 12207 (2017) standard and is divided into six sub-ontologies about:

- testing process (e.g. testing life cycle models);
- testing phase (e.g. unit testing, integration testing, regression testing);
- testing artefact (e.g. test documents, test diagrams, test cases, test requirements, drivers and stubs, artefacts under tests);
- testing resource (e.g. human resource, hardware resource, software resource including testing tools);
- testing procedure (e.g. testing methods, testing guidances, testing techniques);
- testing step (e.g. test planning, test case design, test execution, test analysis).

That leads to a total of 52 ontological terms and first-order-logic axioms that cover the different aspects involved in the testing activity, such as techniques and criteria, human and organisational resources, and automated tools.

## Example 3. Software Test Ontology Integrated ontology

The **Software Test Ontology Integrated (SwTO[I])** (Bezerra et al., 2009) extracted software test knowledge from the Software Engineering Body of Knowledge (SWEBOK) (Bourque and Fairley, 2014) and has formalised 194 terms and axioms for use case concepts, in order to help build quality software with reduced cost, time, and effort.

In particular, SwTO[I] has a focus on **Linux** testing and thus contains concepts of both the Linux operating system domain and the Linux software testing domain. Indeed, SwTO[I] integrates the operating system ontology (OSOnto) and the software test ontology (SwTO). OSOnto represents concepts of the Linux operating system domain and reuses the Basic Linux Ontology (BLO) (2021). SwTO deals with the Linux software testing domain and is based on the Linux Test Project (LTP) (2021), which is a repository with scripts, tools, and more than 3,000 test cases, but with deficient documentation.

Hence, SwTO[I] aims to supply a formal vocabulary of the Linux-test domain, while also providing the semantic record of the systematic test elaborations' criteria as well as the semantic record of the test designers' knowledge.

## Example 4. Reference Ontology on Software Testing ontology

The **Reference Ontology on Software Testing (ROoST)** (Ferreira de Souza et al., 2017) is a mature ontology, which purpose is manifold. Indeed, ROoST establishes a common conceptualisation about the software testing domain, in order to define a common vocabulary of the testing domain for people involved in testing, to structure testing knowledge repositories, to annotate testing knowledge items, and to make a search for relevant information easier.

It also provides computerised support for the tasks of acquiring, processing, analysing, and disseminating testing knowledge for reuse.

ROoST has been built on the ISO/IEC/IEEE 29119-2013 standard (parts 1, 2, 3 and 4), the IEEE 829-2008 standard, and the SWEBOK (Bourque and Fairley, 2014). It has defined 45 terms and axioms in first-order logic and has used the UFO upper ontology as well as interconnected domain-related ontology patterns, which concepts were extended to the testing domain. Thence, ROoST is composed of four sub-ontologies for:

- testing process and activities (e.g. test planning, test case design, test coding, test execution, test result analysis) (Black et al., 2012) reusing the process and activity execution (PAE) pattern;

- testing artefacts (e.g. test plan, test procedure, test case, test results) reusing work product participation (WPPA) pattern;

- testing techniques (e.g. black-box testing techniques, white-box testing techniques, defect-based testing techniques, model-based testing techniques) reusing the procedure participation (PRPA) pattern;

- testing team and environment (e.g. hardware resources, software resources, human resources) reusing the human resource participation (HRPA) and resource participation (RPA) patterns.

### Example 5. AI-T ontology

**Artificial-intelligence-based-system testing ontology (AI-T)** (Olszewska, 2020) is a rich software-testing ontology that is especially dedicated to AI-based systems' testing and contains 708 terms and 706 axioms so far.

This ontology covers both the software testing domain and AI domain, encompassing ethical and explainable AI. AI-T body of knowledge includes ISO/IEC/IEEE 29119-2013 standard (Parts 1, 2, 3, and 4), ISO/IEC/IEEE 24765:2017 standard, IEEE 70xx standards such as 7001 (Winfield et al., 2021), 7010 (2020), as well as SWEBOK (Bourque and Fairley, 2014) and ISTQB (2021).

An excerpt of the encoded concepts and properties of the AI-T ontology is presented in Figure 6.1.

AI-T ontology main concepts have been identified as software testing strategy, software testing process, software testing documentation, software testing levels, software testing techniques, software testing types, software testing artefacts, software testing measures, software testing activities, stakeholders, and environment.

## TRENDS IN ONTOLOGY-DRIVEN SOFTWARE TESTING

To conclude this chapter, it is important to discuss the past, present, and future trends in ontological software testing.

### Ontology requirements

The scope of the ontologies for software testing is evolving; so are the requirements. Therefore, ontology's requirement elicitation and analysis is an important task in the ontological engineering process (Bayat et al., 2016). This can be done using **Unified Modeling Language (UML)** (Kogut et al., 2002). Hence, the current key requirements of ontologies for software testing can be summarised in the UML use case diagram, as presented in Figure 6.2.

The past requirements of the first software testing ontologies such as ROoST were as follows:

- supporting human learning of the software testing process;
- serving as a basis for structuring and representing knowledge related to software testing;
- standing as a reference model for integrating software tools supporting the testing process;
- acting as a reference model for annotating testing, resources in a semantic documentation approach.

Nowadays, requirements of ontologies for software testing, such as AI-T include:

- supporting human tester(s) in managing software testing;
- helping human testers in testing AI-based software;

# Figure 6.1 A view of AI-T ontology for software testing

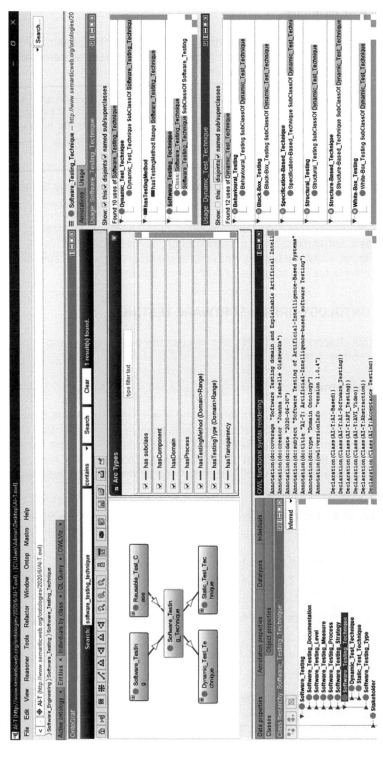

- guiding intelligent agent(s) in generating/reusing test cases;
- facilitating intelligent agent(s)' learning about software testing;
- aiding collaborative mixed human–intelligent agent teams in testing software agents.

These requirements can be expanded over time, as the systems and software become more complex to test (Olszewska, 2019a).

---

**Figure 6.2 UML use case diagram of new-generation ontologies for software testing**

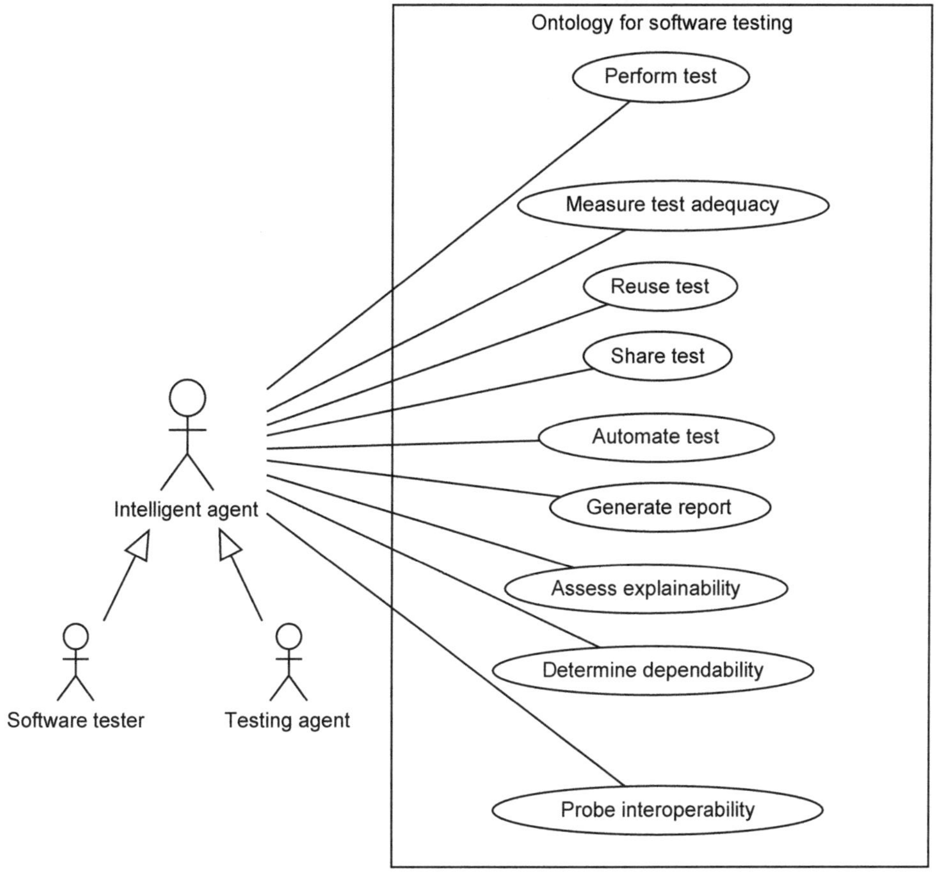

## Ontology explainability

Ontologies are traditionally formalised using logic axioms, allowing **logic-based formal reasoning**. Therefore, such logic-based ontologies are intrinsically explainable. Thence, they constitute a transparent AI technology that is appropriate for applications involving autonomous systems (Olszewska, 2018c) and robotics (Olivares-Alarcos et al., 2019).

Furthermore, these logical ontological approaches are usually built manually and collaboratively by both domain experts and ontologists (Bermejo-Alonso et al., 2018), for example following **the ontological standard development life cycle (ROSADev)** process (Olszewska et al., 2018), and leading to ontological standards such as the 2021 IEEE Standard Association Award-winning IEEE 7007-2021 Ontological Standard for Ethically Driven Robotics and Automation System (Olszewska et al., 2020).

Ontologies can also be used in conjunction with ML. Indeed, ML techniques such as **clustering** (Maedche and Staab, 2004) can help the automatic extraction of ontological concepts from bodies of knowledge. More recently, **deep learning** (Petrucci et al., 2016) has been applied to automatically identify ontological axioms in datasets.

On the other hand, deep recursive neural networks (Hohenecker and Lukasiewicz, 2020) have been used to perform automated reasoning on ontologies. This novel approach for ontology reasoning, which is based on deep learning rather than logic-based formal reasoning, has shown promising performance. However, traditional logic-based ontologies that rely on classical logical reasoners allow automated reasoning while providing transparency (Dragoni et al., 2020), which is sought after by users and experts, including system and software engineers, designers, developers, and testers.

## Ontology applications

With the growing number and complexity of intelligent systems and intelligent agents – all relying on software, whether integrated, distributed, or cloud-based – new techniques to test such systems and software are necessary (Olszewska, 2019b). Ontologies are an AI technology that brings a solution for software testing of such complex, heterogeneous systems.

Indeed, ontologies aim to create a common knowledge representation of a domain that is shared by a group of intelligent agents (Chari et al., 2020), whether humans or not. An ontology generates thus a formal conceptualisation of this shared domain, providing an interoperable system and allowing automated reasoning on it (Tudorache, 2020).

For example in Industry 4.0, interoperability contributes to build a trusted environment in a manufacturing system, in which information is accurately and swiftly shared among machines and humans, resulting in a cost-saving operation with higher productivity (Koh et al., 2019). Hence, ontologies for Industry 4.0 (Sampath Kumar et al., 2019) capture cutting-edge domains such as the smart manufacturing domain and represent this domain knowledge in an unambiguous, interoperable, explainable and reusable way that allows, among others, automated testing and the setting of the foundation for smart manufacturing digital twin modelling.

In particular, to perform ontologically driven testing of complex, heterogeneous, and autonomous systems, software testers can use core ontologies for robotics and automation, such as CORA, as well as upper ontologies about the world knowledge representation, such as SUMO, together with more specialised ontologies that formalise the software testing domain, such as AI-T software-testing ontology. Furthermore, when the complex system under test evolves in a smart environment, additional domain ontologies developed for smart applications (e.g. smart manufacturing, smart cities, etc.)

could be reused in conjunction with other available I4.0 ontologies, for example dedicated to the **Internet of Things (IoT)** (Ma et al., 2014).

## SUMMARY

In summary, ontologies for software testing present an **agent-centric approach**. On one hand, they help to automate the testing of software and, on the other hand, they enable the testing of AI-based systems.

Besides, ontologies are both explainable and interoperable. They allow a **trustworthy** collaboration between heterogeneous intelligent agents such as humans, autonomous systems, intelligent agents, or systems of systems. That is particularly useful in the context of software and system testing. Indeed, such an ontological approach can be used by intelligent agents such as software testers performing smart system testing; autonomous systems seeking self-repairs; or intelligent systems with a human-in-the-loop testing.

Moreover, ontologies provide a **modular** and reusable approach for software testing, that can be integrated within other source code, for example through the use of OWL API – a Java API for OWL 2.0 ontologies – or JSON-LD – a lightweight syntax to serialise Linked Data in JSON – and/or that can assist **Testing-as-a-Service (TaaS)** platforms.

# 7 SHIFTING RIGHT INTO THE METAVERSE WITH DIGITAL TWIN TESTING

## Jonathon Wright

Shift right with digital twin testing means harnessing the power of analytics and autonomics to learn from the real world dynamically. Faced with volatile systemic failure models, digital interfaces need to be highly robust, work through numerous endpoints and process vast volumes of structured and unstructured data. Although adopting continual delivery and testing will help to enable agility, automation is generally powered by static rules using traditional scripting and orchestration. These approaches have a high maintenance overhead in order to keep up to date with changing requirements. The recent advent of predictive analytics and cognitive engineering technologies such as AIOps has opened up the possibility of pushing adaptive automation to self-healing and self-configuration, within evolving real-world situations.

## THE SHIFT-RIGHT APPROACH TO TESTING

Increasing the benefits of learning by shifting the focus more to the right-hand side of the information systems design and testing cycle.

To better understand what shift right is, let us first explore what shift left is all about. Shift left refers to the traditional sequential design techniques of waterfall/V-model methodologies (i.e. requirement analysis, design, testing, then implementation), to the more recent focus of iterative agile design principles.

Recent approaches in systems design and testing tend to still be focused on tackling issues during the design phase rather than later in the life cycle (e.g. root cause analysis and the Pareto principle to find and eliminate the sources of the greatest number of defects) (see Figure 7.1), the intention being to reduce the costs that would otherwise arise from rework following changes.

When an information system or a piece of software is designed by trying to figure out as much as possible what would be best for the users based on testing every possible way that it could fail has an effect on the early design and testing phase, it can be called shifting to the left of the IT systems or software development cycle. Hence, the term shifting left is used to describe such practices.

Shifting left relates to the finding and removal of defects as close as possible to the point of introduction. This approach tends to shift the focus of time and effort towards the early design and testing phases, that is, shifting to the left of the systems or software development cycle.

**Figure 7.1 Shifting left and shifting right**

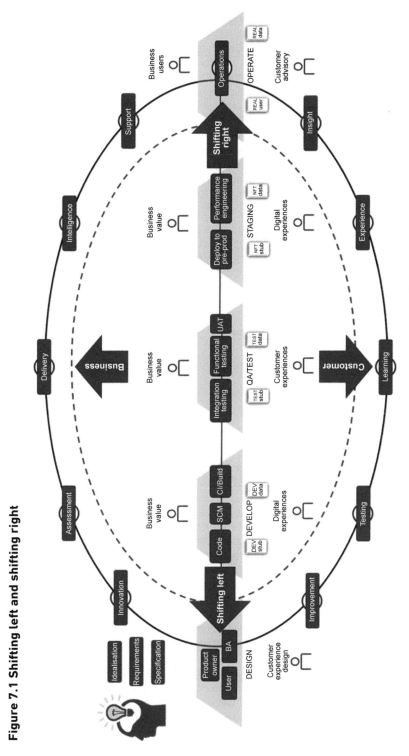

Note: BA = business analyst; CI = continuous integration; DEV = development; NFT = non-functional testing; pre-prod = pre-production; QA = quality assurance; SCM = source code management; UAT = user acceptance testing.

## Contrasting shifting right with shifting left

With shifting right, rather than trying to identify the issues that could arise early on in the development and testing phases, we quickly develop and gain customer feedback sooner rather than spending excessive time on testing, thus shifting more to the right-hand side of the development and testing cycle.

Shifting right puts more weight on the learning aspect and the continual evolution of systems design and testing. After deploying the system or software, user experiences and other data are used as feedback. This feedback loop connects what the system or the software was designed for, to what is actually happening in the real world, in order to get a better understanding of the essential changes needed.

Shifting right relates to developing systems iteratively by focusing on learning rapidly from customer feedback. This approach focuses on quickly developing and releasing it to the users or focus groups to minimise the total testing time. Such a methodology is shifted more to the right-hand side of the development and testing life cycle.

## COGNITIVE ENGINEERING PRINCIPLES

Cognitive engineering software development principles can be considered as a trifecta of the following:

(i) **Thinking segment**. Where we model something and expect it to behave in a particular manner.

(ii) **Creating segment**. Create according to the thinking aspect.

(iii) **Learning segment**. Learning with the help of operational tools and mapping if the created product or service has managed to deliver as predicted in step (i) (Figure 7.2).

This traditional linear process now incorporates the feedback loop, feeding back data from events in the real world. By using a shift-right approach, the learning aspect can be achieved earlier on, and developers can start getting feedback on the system or software development much earlier in the life cycle, thereby saving considerable time for overall development and testing.

In other words, shifting right is a process of learning from the right-hand side or the user journey of the information system or software and using the feedback data to evolve smarter development and testing techniques that can help developers and testers understand potential issues that could arise before they occur.

But how can testers identify the potential issues that could arise with such a developed system? A plain explanation would be to say by looking at it with a more OpsDev approach, compared to the conventional DevOps approach, with the help of artificial intelligence, machine learning and deep learning technologies.

**Figure 7.2 Cognitive engineering** (Source: J. Wright, in Kinsbruner, 2020)

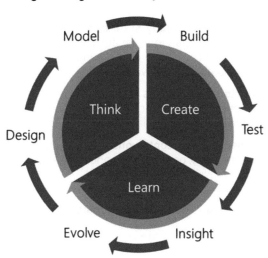

We are all familiar with the conventional software development cycle and the part played by DevOps, best described as enabling 'Dev-centric Ops-capabilities', where the actual true value should be OpsDev, 'Ops-centric Dev-enablement' collaboration. This can be achieved by providing improved insight into the operational space; these tools should not be limited only to the production space. Similar or better tools could be utilised to learn more about the behaviour of the software that is being built under the shift-right discipline.

## Cognitive engineering disciplines

Cognitive engineering is a method of study using the concepts behind cognitive behavioural psychology to design and develop engineering systems to support the cognitive processes expected by the users (Wilson et al., 2013). How can cognitive engineering disciplines help to shift right the testing? By leveraging certain heuristics such as:

- **Performance engineering**. The emulation of production loads to determine the performance limitations (or bottlenecks). These tests are carried out to sort out any issues that might transpire under heavy load conditions.

- **Site reliability testing (SRT)**. The focus of real-world testing of software within production. In other words, it is the practice of maintaining the programmable infrastructure and maximising the availability of the workloads that run on it. Site reliability testers blur the boundaries between testing within the software development life cycle (SDLC) and operations excellence, by applying a software testing mindset to IT operations management (ITOM).

- **Chaos engineering**. The discipline of experimenting on a software system in production in order to build confidence in the system's capability to withstand unpredictable conditions.

The 'thinking segment' in Figure 7.3 defines the 'experiment' and proves the 'hypothesis' of the behaviours, sharing the 'Principles of Chaos Engineering' (2019):

- **Build a hypothesis around steady state behaviour.** Focus on the measurable output of a system, rather than internal attributes of the system, by focusing on systemic behaviour patterns during experiments, verifying that the system does work, rather than validating how it works.

- **Introduce real-world events.** Chaos variants reflect real-world events. Prioritise events either by potential impact or estimated frequency. Any event capable of disrupting a steady state is a potential variant in an experiment.

- **Automate experiments to run continuously.** Build into the production system the ability to drive observability, orchestration and analysis.

---

**Figure 7.3 Cognitive thinking: 'The Digital Manifesto'** (Source: Wright, 2016b)

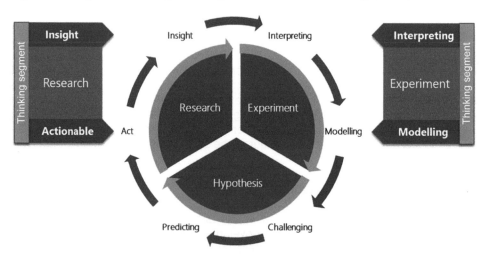

Chaos engineering is the discipline of experimenting on a software system in production in order to build confidence in the system's capability to withstand turbulent and unexpected conditions (Principles of Chaos Engineering, 2019).

We can take these disciplines and apply them to the development of cognitive platforms such as those with artificial intelligence, machine learning and deep learning. The true power of cognitive engineering is that we can prove a hypothesis rapidly using these disciplines. This is where the real science behind modelling is the workload; volumetrics models help us to understand the real-world user journeys and allow us to create realistic load profiles that then can be run against target predefined system states.

**Figure 7.4 Cognitive Learning – 'Digital Evolution, Over Revolution'** (Source: Wright, 2017)

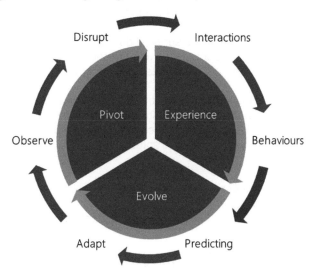

Cognitive engineering disciplines in collaboration with application performance management (APM) platforms, when combined with intelligent operations (AIOps), can help systems designers to identify when a system is going to break before it happens.

SRT enables observability and testability of a hyper-baselined system, that is, utilising multidimensional transactional datasets (for example combining time series data with streaming data services, such as the TICK stack) (Figure 7.4). This enables realistic or synthetically generated loads to be measured, and used to prove the hypothesis of a system or application.

## DIGITAL TWIN CONCEPT IN SHIFTING RIGHT

The complex nature of modern software development often results in layers of abstraction, for example the hardware abstraction layer (HAL) hides the complexity of hardware design from software engineers. The same is true with systems of systems; the concept of a digital twin allows the abstraction of system thinking to make it explainable and understandable to non-technical subject matter experts.

Digital twin is the generation or collection of digital data representing a physical or virtual object. The concept of digital twin has its roots in engineering and the creation of engineering drawings or graphics. Digital twins are the outcome of continual improvement in the creation of product design and engineering activities.

NASA's Apollo 13 mission can be considered as the first time the digital twin concept was used to safely return astronauts to Earth.

After a successful launch, Apollo 13 suffered damage to its main engine due to an explosion in the oxygen tank upon jettisoning the service module. This resulted in a life-threatening leak from the astronauts' oxygen supply.

Mission control had to quickly dispatch all available ground resources to bring the astronauts home. With the help of other astronauts on the ground using simulators, NASA replicated the situation taking place in space nearly 200,000 miles away from Earth and managed to figure out a solution to return the astronauts to Earth successfully.

They created a virtual representation of the crippled spacecraft and ran simulations on that digital twin to better understand how to fix the damage before applying the changes made in the simulated environment to the actual one (Ritchson, 2021).

## CASE STUDY: HELPING THE COMMUNITY STAY SAFE DURING THE PANDEMIC

Figure 7.5 depicts a COVID-19 dashboard taken on 14 February 2021, provided by Todd DeCapua (member of the 'Splunk for Good' team).

In 2020, Rob Tiffany shared the concept of how digital twins could be our best weapon in fighting the COVID-19 pandemic. This can be seen on YouTube at: https://youtu.be/XKINvqiTgxQ.

The digital twin approach helped to reduce the spread of COVID-19 during the pandemic by supporting the testing of both the global positioning system (GPS) and Google Apple Exposure Notifications (GAEN) contact tracing platforms. By working closely with Google and Apple, MIT were able to incorporate Bluetooth data instead of relying on GPS data, so that Bluetooth could be used as a proximity sensor when two individuals (or devices) interact. As a result of this collaboration came the idea of applying digital twins to help solve the contact tracing testing challenge.

Since early 2020, I have been collaborating directly with MIT, leading the quality assurance and testing efforts for the COVID PathCheck Foundation (n.d.). This focused on creating a more efficient contact tracing solution than the manual process used by other health officials at that time, which involved asking individuals where they have been, who they encountered, and so on for the past few days. Their manual approach was prone to many deficiencies as it relied heavily on an individual's memory of the places they had visited.

The motive behind using such a concept in the contact tracing project was to increase the accuracy of the app by reducing the number of false positive alerts. When the whole

**Figure 7.5 COVID-19 patterns and trends, 2021** (Source: Splunk for Good)

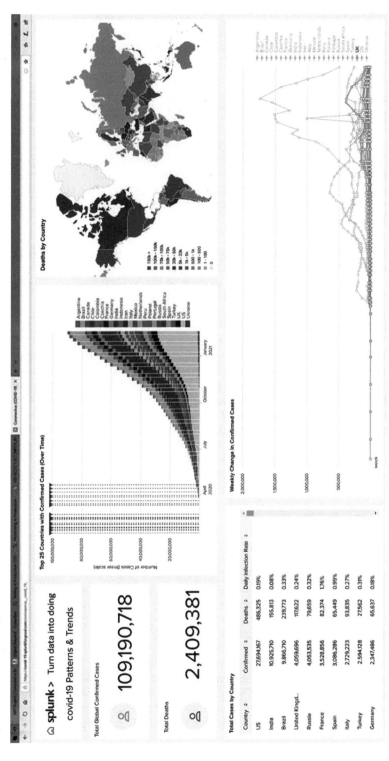

world was affected by the spread of COVID-19, countries were in dire need of an effective solution for contact tracing. Dedicating a lot of time to consider all possible outcomes before an app can be made available was not a feasible solution.

The British government started working on developing a mobile app to alert people to possible exposure to the virus, aiming to reduce the spread of the virus. They tested the app using real people walking around with smartphones to simulate real-world interactions. This shift-left approach consumed a disproportionate amount of time beforehand and resulted in the health authorities being unable to deliver a workable solution in time (Ward, 2020). This was a classic example of where a shift-right approach could have minimised the time constraints and enabled a practical and efficient contact tracing app to be developed more quickly.

Our shift-right approach applied the digital twin semantic to represent historical location data of users who have experienced symptoms, are infected or have recovered. After developing the app, we created a model (shown on the left-hand side of Figure 7.6) of the mobile app (shown on the right-hand side).

Now, let us say that people in London on a particular day are represented by pins as shown in Figure 7.7. The ones marked in the darker colour represent a person infected with COVID-19. There are relatively few darker dots. Some of these individuals may be driving in cars, taking the bus or self-isolating in their homes. Those driving in the confined space of their cars pose no risk of infecting a person outside the car until they get out of their car and go into an enclosed space, so the app does not necessarily need to trigger an alarm. The consequences of such false positives include people having to self-quarantine for no actual risk of infection.

This is where we can leverage machine learning to better understand real-world scenarios and differentiate between a darker dot representing a person driving a car at 6 mph, or a pedestrian walking at 3 mph, compared with someone sitting in a coffee shop in close proximity to other citizens.

By default, since 2017, every Android phone has been effectively tracking and capturing user locations every 5 minutes, whereas Google's location services by default collect 650 data points of locations every 24 hours, resulting in 9,100 data points over a possible 14-day 'incubation' period. It was important to follow a privacy-first approach for our project, which involves the editing out of any personally identifiable data (Collins, 2017). GCHQ and the NHSx app came under fire during field testing of the mobile app on the Isle of Wight; they had been using Google Firebase and telemetry data from real users, thereby highlighting data privacy concerns (Ward, 2020).

By exporting location data from Google Takeout, we were able to obtain the historical GPS data of Android devices (GPS location data logs that are generally available for up to 10 years). The bottom left of Figure 7.8 shows the GPS coordinates. By utilising Google Takeout, we extracted Google users' pre-existing location data to find out what had been happening in the real world. Obtaining GPX (GPS Exchange format) data from

**Figure 7.6 MIT project Safe Paths App: Digital Twin model view**

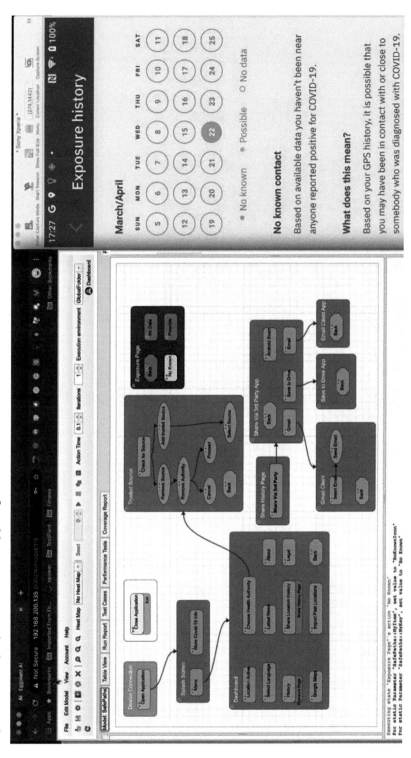

**Figure 7.7 MIT project Safe Places: Redaction Tool**

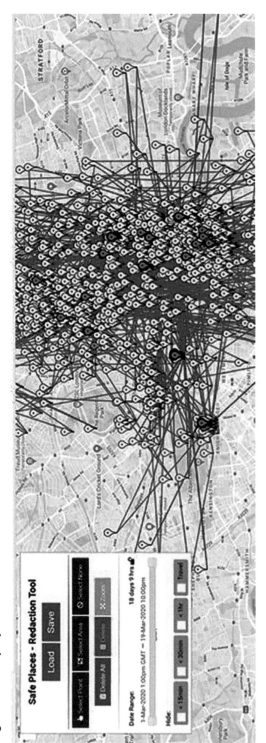

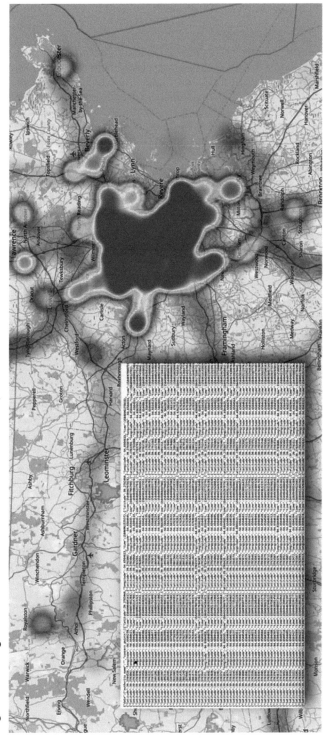

**Figure 7.8 Google Takeout: historical data around Boston, Massachusetts**

hundreds and thousands of users constituted enough big data to warrant the creation of a data lake.

Applying cognitive engineering, we took this data lake and integrated machine learning, AI and deep learning technologies to process the structured GPX data based on schema-based generation (randomised algorithms) and neural networks (natural language processing, generative models) to maintain the statistical properties of location data and to synthesise realistic test data cubes. By using the synthetically generated data and injecting the GPX dataset from the model-based data scenarios into hundreds of real devices, the behaviour of each device exposure notification status could be observed.

## Testing the COVID-19 contract tracing platform

Digital experiences (DX) are when user behaviours are combined with digital interactions. This approach enabled us to better understand what changes need to be made to optimise the user experience of information systems and applications. Within the context of this book, another way to say this is that we can learn from the real world, or the 'right-hand side' (an already available application or information system), and the user interaction information can be fed to a model (a digital twin of the real application).

The MIT project was next launched in Berkeley to help the health officials with contact tracing (Figure 7.9). For it to be successful, we needed real data inputs from people as we could not emulate historical user data. This is an example of where combining crowd testing and the shift-right approach was the best option to successfully test the solution in production.

## CASE STUDY: SMART CITY DATA EXCHANGE – TESTING IN THE METAVERSE

There were a number of similarities between the approaches used for the Copenhagen Smart City Data Exchange and the MIT contact tracing initiatives. The biggest challenge in both projects was the ability to synthetically produce billions of historically accurate position data points and inject location data into GPS in real time.

The Smart City Data Exchange in Copenhagen used location data to help digital citizens become carbon neutral by 2020 (Figure 7.10). A smart city mobile app was rolled out to 38,000 people living and working in Copenhagen.

### Metaverse concept applied to testing in the real world

> **Metaverse** is blurring of the boundaries between technology (i.e. software and physical hardware) and the real world (originating back in 1992 in Neal Stephenson's novel, *Snow Crash*).

As demonstrated in my 2017 TED talk on Cognitive Learning (Figure 7.11), the use of augmented and mixed reality (AR/MR) headsets from Google, Apple and Meta (Zuckerberg,

**Figure 7.9 MIT project Safe Places: Redaction Tool**

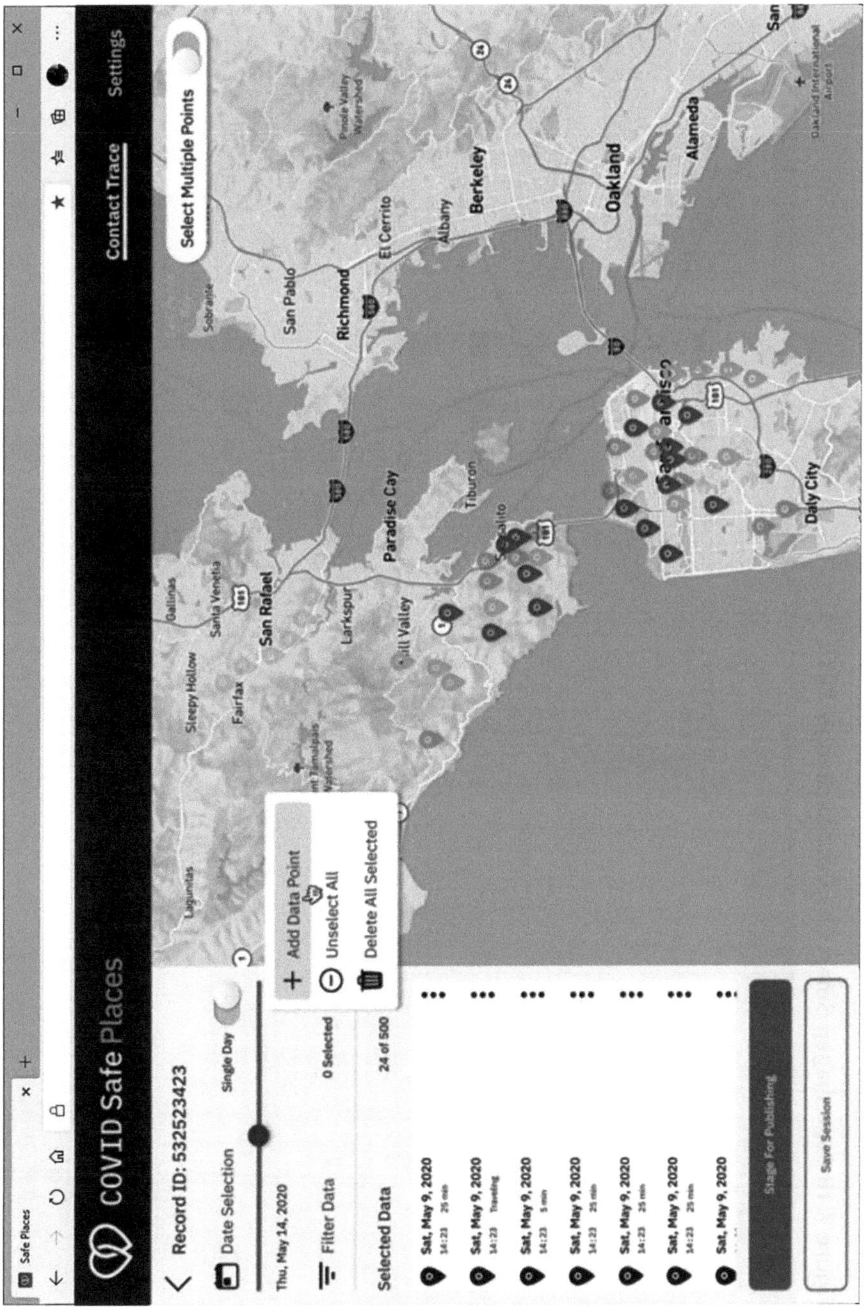

# Figure 7.10 Copenhagen Smart City Data Exchange, 2015

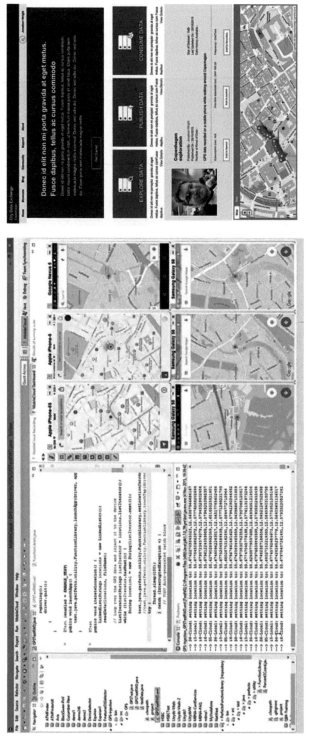

2021) (previously Facebook) overlaid metadata enabling DX interactions with the real world to create a digital-world-that-actually-mirrors-our-own and offering unprecedented interoperability of data and cross sharing through non-fungible tokens (NFTs).

A non-fungible token is a unique digital identifier that cannot be copied, substituted, or subdivided, that is recorded in a blockchain, and that is used to certify authenticity and ownership (as of a specific digital asset and specific rights relating to it) (Merriam-Webster, 2021).

**Figure 7.11 TED talk: Cognitive Learning – 'Digital Evolution, over Revolution', 2017**

The challenge with testing within the metaverse is the ability to identify multi-modal modes of transport used by the citizen in the physical world. These ranged from walking (2–3 mph), cycling (10–12 mph), taking the bus (stopping at various locations), taking the train, or taking the Tube (which can stop recording GPX data at one location and show up at another place). Each mode had a unique footprint that would need to be cross-referenced to identify the type of transportation used.

Going back to the COVID-19 project scenario, we already have the historical data from the mobile devices about where people are most likely to be gathered and the paths they have taken. Therefore, we can predict when and where people are going to be, for instance gathered around a certain area based on historical data. For example, during weekends, there are going to be a lot of people going to the beach; during weekdays there are going to be a lot of people using the commuter services around morning and evening rush hour time. In this way, we can predict where congestion is most likely to occur based on the behavioural data of a lot of people.

This is the same idea behind incorporating machine learning technologies within AIOps with predictive capabilities, by using historical data leveraging time series data.

AIOps uses artificial intelligence to simplify IT operations management and accelerate and automate problem resolution in complex modern IT environments. Such operations tasks include automation, performance monitoring and event correlations, amongst others (IBM Cloud Education, 2020).

## SHIFTING RIGHT INTO THE METAVERSE

It is not uncommon to be awed by the user experience we get from our devices, whether we are using a smartphone, a tablet or any electronic gadget for that matter. This is no different when it comes to applications or information systems. We all like a very user-friendly, rich user experience when we interact with these devices.

However, we are moving further away from pure user experiences (UX) to fully immersive DX. For example, using your mobile phone or smart glasses while on a sightseeing walk, any photos taken are automatically uploaded to the metaverse. Your smart device likely also has associated metadata of GPS location, number of steps you have taken, identity of what was captured, and may even convert your digital media pictures, videos or audio into NFTs, which could be traded and sold on digital marketplaces on a digital ledger like blockchain, all thanks to next generation cognitive engineering capabilities such as computer vision, natural language processing (NLP) and machine learning built into physical edge artificial intelligence-enabled endpoint devices.

If we look at a few examples of how these structured data has been used by platforms to enrich user experiences, such as asking Alexa a question, we are interacting with the device using voice commands and the device is talking to many platforms to find the solution to our inquiry, giving us suggestions based on our likes and dislikes. Video streaming services such as Amazon Prime and Netflix, for instance, might suggest a movie to us based on a movie we watched or an actor we have been interested in recently.

These are all happening without our direct interference, to the betterment of the user experience. Now, imagine hundreds of millions of devices being carried by people on a single day and the amount of such unstructured data gathered from the user experiences. These unstructured data may be rendered useless until they have been extracted, transformed or loaded (ETL) into structured formats or associated metadata, utilising something like a schema registry or knowledge graph to become more context sensitive.

### Gamification, permutations and lessons from Pokémon Go

Going back to the MIT COVID-19 project, user data are based on actual user interactions, that is, real people moving around in the real world with their smart devices. When it comes to a pandemic, using real human beings to gather GPS and Bluetooth information to test an app is not the safest idea because of the risk of these participants getting infected.

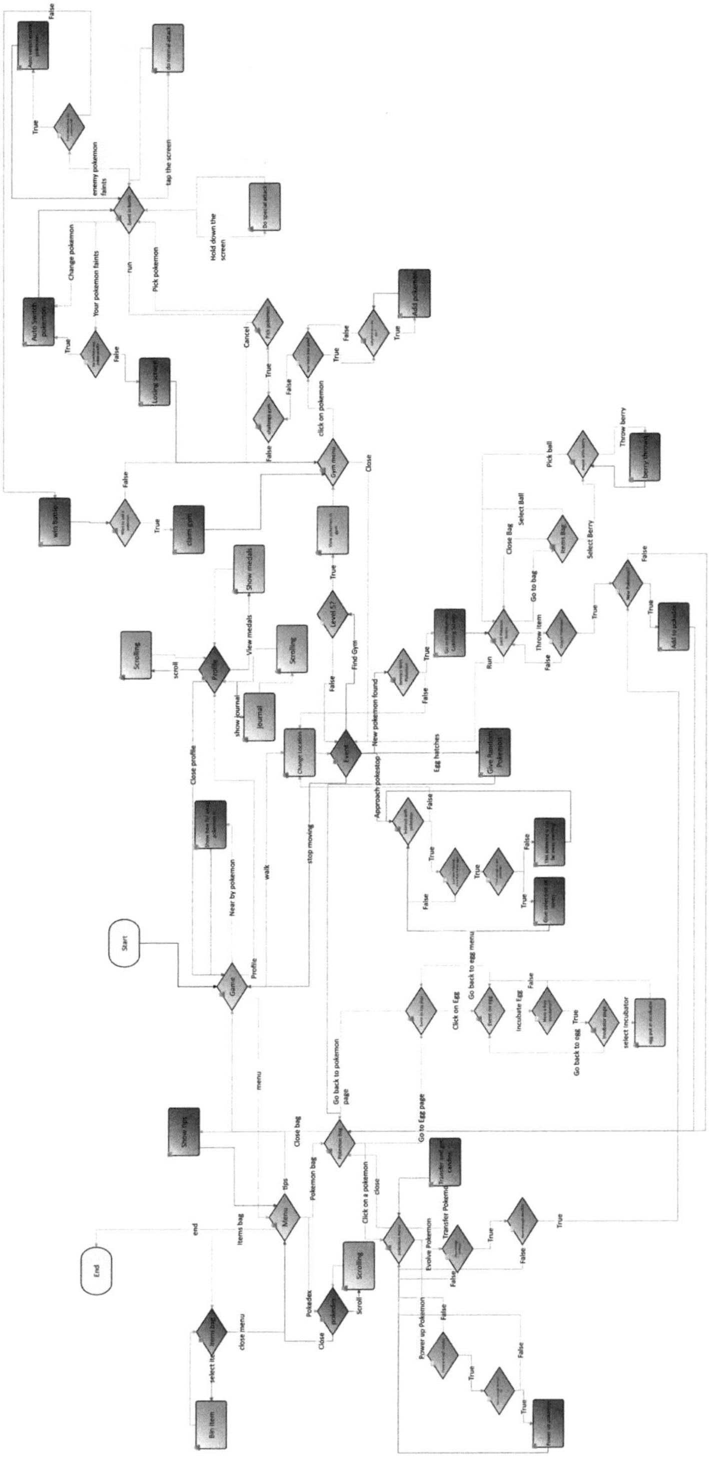

**Figure 7.12 Utilising model-based testing with Pokémon Go** (Source: Wright, 2016a)

# Figure 7.13 Agile Requirements Designer (ArD), 2016, MBT of London Underground

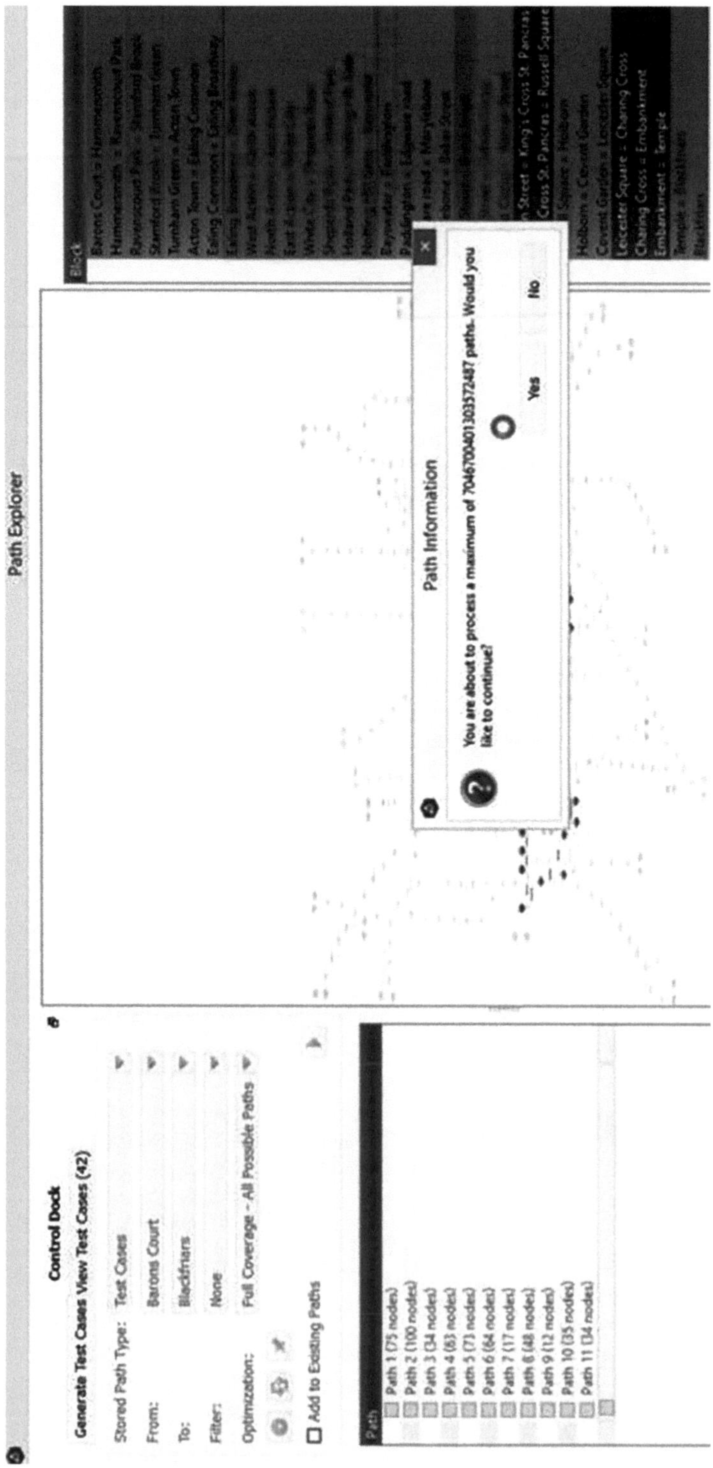

Instead of having real people, we could use location data and inject the locations to simulate visiting those places without having to go there. This is similar to the way people managed to cheat the GPS location-based mobile game Pokémon Go. This game is a fantastic example of augmented reality, gamification and the metaverse as it was intended to be played by the players physically going to places in the real world, unlocking location and time sensitive achievements and catching the Pokémon scattered around the globe.

In Figure 7.12 you can see the Pokémon example utilising model-based testing (MBT). Again, using a similar approach to testing the metaverse, we could magically appear to be at all the physical locations without having to actually be at any of them. This was achieved by combining location data with Google Street View to simulate the camera feed and catch the Pokémon by emulating gestures and digital interactions within the metaverse through augmented reality.

If we assume that we want to go from a point A to a point B in the real world, we have a lot of possible routes to take us to the destination (see Figure 7.13 for possible paths on the London Underground). Considering as many possible real-world variables and their permutations, such as if a person is walking, driving in a car or taking the bus or train, we can simulate near infinite possible digital experiences without physical effort or risk.

## EVOLUTION, OVER REVOLUTION

Human advancements have brought about many revolutionary changes, starting from the first generation of evolution that was the steam-powered revolution, through the second generation that was electric and fossil fuel-powered, into the third generation that is driven by computers, electronics and telecommunications, to the fourth generation, soon to be powered by artificial intelligence. Within these revolutions, design disciplines used for developing computer systems and software have also seen a lot of change over the last few decades.

Back in 1939 Hewlett and Packard spearheaded the design principles used in developing computer systems. The waterfall method is a very linear process and was used to organise the manufacture of hardware products long before it was re-utilised to design software and information systems. Industry moved on, to more iterative methodologies. In the 1960s EVO (short for Evolutionary Project Management) introduced iterative development was first published in 1976 by Tom Gilb, followed by the widely adopted Agile Manifesto, which is now the most common method used in many industries. Although advances have been made in the design and test principles, the learning curve has largely remained on 'shifting left'.

Cognitive learning, on the other hand, is a shift-right emphasis, complementary to conventional shift-left 'design and solution thinking' principles such as LeanUX.

We can also greatly benefit from the recent advances made in fields such as machine learning, artificial intelligence and deep learning, incorporating them into modern day software design and testing of information systems to deliver robust results within rich digital experiences, like the metaverse.

Moving forward, utilising disciplines such as 'shifting right' to introduce 'failing fast and learning rapidly' feedback loops from real-world user journeys and digital experiences, together with the help of machine learning, will help us to predict problems with software and systems being designed and tested.

We will also be able to rapidly change the design and validate the digital twin of the system or software based in real time. Digital experiences such as the metaverse, which blur the boundaries between the real world and technology, can be also tested based on predicted outcomes through cognitive learning capabilities only made possible by machine learning and AI.

## SUMMARY

To reduce the massive upfront development work normally associated with introducing a new software system or solution, in the future we can opt for more rapid prototypes of concepts and the evolution of these ideas. Learning from what is going on in the real world and applying this feedback by shifting right will spearhead this 'Evolution, Over Revolution'.

# REFERENCES

ACLU (2019) 'Facebook agrees to sweeping reforms to curb discriminatory ad targeting practices'. Available from: https://www.aclu.org/press-releases/facebook-agrees-sweeping-reforms-curb-discriminatory-ad-targeting-practices

Al Feel, H. T. and Khafagy, M. H. (2011) 'OCSS: Ontology cloud storage system'. In *Proceedings of the IEEE International Symposium on Network Cloud Computing and Applications*. 9–13.

Ali, M., Sapiezynski, P., Bogen, M., Korolova, A., Mislove, A. and Rieke, A. (2019) 'Discrimination through optimization: How Facebook's ad delivery can lead to biased outcomes'. In *Proceedings of the ACM on Human-Computer Interaction*. 3. 1–30.

Alqahtani, S. S., Eghan, E. E. and Rilling, J. (2017) 'Recovering semantic traceability links between APIs and security vulnerabilities: An ontological modeling approach'. In *Proceedings of the IEEE International Conference on Software Testing, Verification and Validation*. 80–91.

Alzantot, M., Sharma, Y., Elgohary, A., Ho, B-J., Srivastava, M. and Chang, K.-W. (2018) 'Generating natural language adversarial examples'. In *Proceedings of the 2018 Conference on Empirical Methods in Natural Language Processing*. 2890–2896.

Alsudais, A. (2021) 'Incorrect data in the widely used Inside Airbnb dataset'. *Decision Support Systems*, 141. 113453.

Angwin, J., Mattu, S. and Larson, J. (2015) 'The tiger mom tax: Asians are nearly twice as likely to get a higher price from Princeton Review'. Available from: https://www.propublica.org/article/asians-nearly-twice-as-likely-to-get-higher-price-from-princeton-review

Angwin, J., Larson, J., Mattu, S. and Kirchner, L. (2016), 'Machine bias. There is software that is used across the country to predict future criminals. And it is biased against blacks'. Available from: https://www.propublica.org/article/machine-bias-risk-assessments-in-criminal-sentencing

Arpirez, J. C., Corcho, O., Fernandez-Lopez, M. and Gomez-Perez, A. (2001) 'WebODE: A scalable ontological engineering workbench'. In *Proceedings of the ACM International Conference on Knowledge Capture (K-CAP)*. 6–13.

Arya, V., Bellamy, R. K. E., Chen, P.-Y., Dhurandhar, A., Hind, M., Hoffman, S. C., Houde, S., Liao, Q. V., Luss, R., Mojsilović, A., Mourad, S., Pedemonte, P., Raghavendra, R., Richards, J., Sattigeri, P., Shanmugam, K., Singh, M., Varshney, K. R., Wei, D., Zhang, Y. (2019) 'One explanation does not fit all: A toolkit and taxonomy of AI explainability techniques'. Available from: http://arxiv.org/abs/1909.03012

Avdeenko, T. V. and Pustovalova, N. V. (2016) 'The ontology-based approach to support the requirements engineering process'. In *Proceedings of the IEEE International Scientific-Technical Conference on Actual Problems of Electronics Instrument Engineering*. 513–518.

Baader, F., Calvanese, D., McGuinness, D., Nardi, D. and Patel-Schneider, P. (eds) (2003) *The Description Logic Handbook: Theory, Implementation, and Applications*. Cambridge University Press.

Barbosa, E. F., Nakagawa, E. Y. and Maldonado, J. C. (2006) 'Towards the establishment of an ontology of software testing'. In *Proceedings of IEEE International Conference on Software Engineering and Knowledge Engineering (SEKE)*. 522–525.

Basic Linux Ontology (BLO) (2021). Available from: http://wwwis.win.tue.nl/~swale/blo

Bayat, B., Bermejo-Alonso, J., Carbonera, J. L., Facchinetti, T., Fiorini, S. R., Goncalves, P., Jorge, V., Habib, M., Khamis, A., Melo, K., Nguyen, B., Olszewska, J. I., Paull, L., Prestes, E., Ragavan, S. V., Saeedi. S., Sanz, R., Seto, M., Spencer, B., Trentini, M., Vosughi, A. and Li, H. (2016) 'Requirements for building an ontology for autonomous robots'. *Industrial Robot: An International Journal,* 43 (5). 469–480.

BCS (2020a) 'The public don't trust computer algorithms to make decisions about them, survey finds'. Available from: https://www.bcs.org/more/about-us/press-office/press-releases/the-public-don-t-trust-computer-algorithms-to-make-decisions-about-them-survey-finds/

BCS (2020b) 'The exam question: How do we make algorithms do the right thing?' Available from: https://www.bcs.org/media/6135/algorithms-report-2020.pdf

Beizer, B. (1990) *Software Testing Techniques*. Van Nostrand Reinhold.

Bermejo-Alonso, J., Chibani, A., Goncalves, P., Li, H., Jordan, S., Olivares, A., Olszewska, J. I., Prestes, E., Rama Fiorini, S. and Sanz, R. (2018) 'Collaboratively working towards ontology-based standards for robotics and automation'. In *IEEE International Conference on Intelligent Robots and Systems (IROS)*. 79.

Berrani, S., Yachir, A., Djemaa, B. and Aissani, M. (2018) 'Extended multi-agent system based service composition in the Internet of Things'. In *Proceedings of the IEEE International Conference on Pattern Analysis and Intelligent Systems*. 1–8.

Bertrand, M. and Mullainathan, S. (2004) 'Are Emily and Greg more employable than Lakisha and Jamal? A field experiment on labor market discrimination'. *The American Economic Review*, 94. 991–1013.

Bettenburg, N., Premraj, R., Zimmermann, T. and Kim, S. (2008) 'Duplicate bug reports considered harmful ... really?' In *Proceedings of the IEEE International Conference on Software Maintenance (ICSM)*. 337–345. DOI: 10.1109/ICSM.2008.4658082

Bezerra, D., Costa, A. and Okada, K. (2009) 'SwTOⁱ (Software Test Ontology Integrated) and its application in Linux test'. In *Proceedings of IEEE International Workshop on Ontology, Conceptualization and Epistemology for Information Systems, Software Engineering and Service Science*. 25–36.

Bickel, P., Hammel, E. and O'Connell, J. (1975) 'Sex bias in graduate admissions: Data from Berkeley'. *Science*, 187 (4175). 398–404.

Binas, J., Neil, D., Liu, S.-C. and Delbruck, T. (2017) 'DDD17: End-to-end DAVIS driving dataset'. Available from: https://arxiv.org/abs/1711.01458

Black, R. (2015) 'Dimensions of test coverage'. RBCS. Available from: https://rbcs-us.com/site/assets/files/1222/dimensions-of-test-coverage.pdf

Black, R., Van Veenendaal, E. and Graham, D. (2012) *Foundations of Software Testing – ISTQB Certification*. CENGAGE Learning.

Boardman, J. and Sauser, B. (2006) 'System of Systems: The meaning of'. In *Proceedings of the IEEE/SMC International Conference on System of Systems Engineering*. 118–123.

Bonferroni, C. E. (1936) 'Teoria statistica delle classi e calcolo delle probabilità'. *Pubblicazioni del R. Istituto Superiore di Scienze Economiche e Commerciali di Firenze*, 8. 3–62.

Bourque, P. and Fairley, R. E. (2014) *SWEBOK: Guide to Software Engineering Body of Knowledge*, 3rd ed., IEEE.

Breck, E., Cai, S., Nielsen, E., Salib, M. and Sculley, D. (2017) 'The ML test score: A rubric for ML production readiness and technical debt reduction'. In *Proceedings of the IEEE International Conference on Big Data (Big Data)*. 1123–1132. DOI: 10.1109/BigData.2017.8258038

Caliskan, A., Bryson, J. and Narayanan, A. (2017) 'Semantics derived automatically from language corpora contain human-like biases'. *Science*, 356. 183–186.

Campos, H., Acacio, C., Braga, R., Araujo, M. A. P., David, J. M. N. and Campos, F. (2017) 'Regression tests provenance data in the continuous software engineering context'. In *Proceedings of the IEEE Brazilian Symposium on Systematic and Automated Software Testing*. 1–6.

Chari, S., Seneviratne, O., Gruen, D. M., Foreman, M. A., Das, A. K. and McGuinness, D. L. (2020) 'Explanation ontology: A model of explanations for user-centered AI'. In *Proceedings of the International Semantic Web Conference (ISWC)*. 228–243.

Chaudhuri, A., Smith, A. L., Gardner, A., Gu, L., Salem, M. B. and Lévesque, M. (2018) 'Regulatory frameworks relating to data privacy and algorithmic decision making in the context of emerging standards on algorithmic bias'. In *Thirty-fifth Conference on Neural Information Processing Systems*. 6.

Chen, P. and Xi, A. (2020) 'Research on industrial software testing knowledge database based on ontology'. In *Proceedings of the IEEE International Conference on Dependable Systems and Their Applications*. 425–429.

Clarke, E. M., Klieber, W., Nováček, M. and Zuliani, P. (2012) 'Model checking and the state explosion problem'. In B. Meyer and M. Nordio (eds). *Tools for Practical Software Verification. LASER 2011. Lecture Notes in Computer Science*, vol. 7682. Springer. DOI: 10.1007/978-3-642-35746-6_1

Clarke, G. M., Anderson, C., Pettersson, F., Cardon, L., Morris, A. and Zondervan, K. (2011) 'Basic statistical analysis in genetic case-control studies'. *Nature Protocols*, 6 (2). 121–133.

Clean Code Developer (n.d.) 'Clean code initiative'. Available from: https://clean-code-developer.de

CMS Collaboration (2012) 'Observation of a new boson at a mass of 125 GeV with the CMS experiment at the LHC'. *Physics Letters B,* 716 (1). 30–61.

Cohn, M. (2009) *Succeeding with Agile*. Addison-Wesley Professional.

Collins, K. (2017) 'Google collects Android users' locations even when location services are disabled'. Quartz. Available from: https://qz.com/1131515/google-collects-android-users-locations-even-when-location-services-are-disabled/

Creel, K. A. (2020) 'Transparency in complex computational systems'. *Philosophy of Science*, 87 (4). 709–729.

Dal Pozzolo, A., Boracchi, G., Caelen, O., Alippi, C. and Bontempi, G. (2015) 'Credit card fraud detection and concept-drift adaptation with delayed supervised information'. In *Proceedings of the IEEE International Joint Conference on Neural Networks (IJCNN)*. 1–8. DOI: 10.1109/IJCNN.2015.7280527

Da Silva, J. P. S., DallOglio, P., Coelho Da Silva Pinto, S. C., Bittencourt, I. I. and Sardi Mergen, S. L. (2015) 'OntoQAI: An ontology to support quality assurance inspections'. In *Proceedings of the IEEE Brazilian Symposium on Software Engineering*. 11–20.

Davenport, J. (In press) Dataset for chapter 'Quality and Bias'. University of Bath Research Data Archive. DOI: 10.15125/BATH-01099

Davis, R., Shrobe, H. and Szolovits, P. (1993) 'What is a knowledge representation?' *AI Magazine*, 14 (1). 17–33.

de Almeida Falbo, R., Cruz Natali, A. C., Gomes Mian, P., Bertollo, G. and Borges Ruy, F. (2003) 'ODE: Ontology-based software development environment'. *CACIC*. 1124–1135.

Descriptive Ontology for Linguistic and Cognitive Engineering (DOLCE) (2021). Available from: www.loa.istc.cnr.it/dolce/overview.html

Dietz, J. and Mulder, H. (2020) *Enterprise Ontology*. Springer.

Ding, L., Finin, T., Joshi, A., Pan, R., Cost, R. S., Peng, Y., Reddivari, P., Doshi, V. C. and Sachs, J. (2004) 'Swoogle: A semantic web search and metadata engine'. In *Proceedings of the ACM Conference on Information and Knowledge Management*. 652–659.

Dragoni, M., Donadello, I. and Eccher, C. (2020) 'Explainable AI meets persuasiveness: Translating reasoning results into behavioral change advice'. *Artificial Intelligence in Medicine*, 105. 1–17.

Dunn, O. J. (1961) 'Multiple comparisons among means'. *Journal of the American Statistical Association*, 56 (293). 52–64.

Edelman, B. G., Luca, M. and Svirsky, D. (2016) 'Racial discrimination in the sharing economy: Evidence from a field experiment.' Available from: https://hbswk.hbs.edu/item/racial-discrimination-in-the-sharing-economy-evidence-from-a-field-experiment

European Court of Justice (2011) Association Belge des Consommateurs Test-Achats ASBL and Others v Conseil des ministres. Available from: http://curia.europa.eu/juris/liste.jsf?td=ALL&language=en&jur=C,T,F&parties=test%20achats

European Parliament (2016) Regulation (EU) 2016/679 of the European Parliament and of the Council on the protection of natural persons with regard to the processing of personal data and on the free movement of such data. Available from: https://eur-lex.europa.eu/eli/reg/2016/679/oj

European Parliament (2021) Proposal for a Regulation laying down harmonised rules on artificial intelligence. Available from: https://digital-strategy.ec.europa.eu/en/library/proposal-regulation-laying-down-harmonised-rules-artificial-intelligence

Feldmann, S., Roeschm S., Legat, C. and Vogel-Heuser, B. (2014) 'Keeping requirements and test cases consistent: Towards an ontology-based approach'. In *Proceedings of the IEEE International Conference on Industrial Informatics (INDIN)*. 726–732.

Fernandez, M., Gomez-Perez, A. and Juristo, N. (1997) 'Methontology: From ontological art towards ontological engineering'. In *Proceedings of the AAAI Spring Symposium Series*. 33–40.

Ferreira de Souza, E., de Almeida Falbo, R. and Vijaykumar, N. L. (2013) 'Ontologies in software testing: A systematic literature review'. In *Proceedings of the Seminar on Ontology Research in Brazil*. 71–82.

Ferreira de Souza, E., de Almeida Falbo, R. and Vijaykumar, N. L. (2017) 'ROoST: Reference ontology on software testing'. *Applied Ontology*, 12 (1). 59–90.

Fiorini, S., Bermejo-Alonso, J., Goncalves, P., Pignaton de Freitas, E., Olivares, A., Olszewska, J. I., Prestes, E., Schlenoff, C., Ragavan, S. V., Redfield, S., Spencer, B., and Li, H. (2017) 'A suite of ontologies for robotics and automation'. *IEEE Robotics and Automation Magazine*, 24 (1). 8–11.

Fraser, G. (n.d.). Available from: https://www.evosuite.org/

Freitas, A. and Vieira, R. (2014) 'An ontology for guiding performance testing'. In *Proceedings of the IEEE/WIC/ACM International Joint Conferences on Web Intelligence (WI) and Intelligent Agent Technologies (IAT)*. 400–407.

Gebru, T., Morgenstern, J., Vecchione, B., Vaughan, J. W., Wallach, H., Daumé III, H. and Crawford, K. (2021) 'Datasheets for datasets'. *Communications of the ACM*, 64 (12). 86–92.

Gilvoich, T. and Griffin, D. (2010) 'Judgement and decision-making'. In S. T. Fiske, D. T. Gilbert and Lindzey, G. (eds). *Handbook of Social Psychology*, vol. 1. John Wiley & Sons. 542–589.

Gladwell, M. (2021) 'I love you Waymo'. Revisionist History podcast. Available from: http://podcasts.pushkin.fm/revisionist-history-waymo?sid=mg&c=2_SiuQY8fGIlo_E3KAHK-g&h=b8c24575b15cc6ec7

Glimm, B., Horrocks, I., Motik, B., Stoilos, G. and Wang, Z. (2014) 'HermiT: An OWL 2 reasoner'. *Journal of Automated Reasoning*, 53 (3). 245–269.

Gomez-Perez, A., Fernandez-Lopez, M. and Corcho, O. (2004) *Ontological Engineering*. Springer-Verlag.

Google (2021) Machine learning glossary. Available from: https://developers.google.com/machine-learning/glossary/#r

Gordon, P. M. K., Barker, K. and Sensen, C. W. (2010) 'Programming-by-example meets the semantic web: Using ontologies and web services to close the semantic gap'. In *Proceedings of the IEEE Symposium on Visual Languages and Human-Centric Computing*. 133–140.

Griffor, E. R., Greer, C., Wollman, D. A. and Burns, M. J. (2017) Framework for cyber-physical systems: Volume 2, Working group reports. NIST SP 1500-202. National Institute of Standards and Technology. DOI: 10.6028/NIST.SP.1500-202

Gross, F., Fraser, G. and Zeller, A. (2012) 'Search-based system testing: High coverage, no false alarms'. In *Proceedings of the ACM International Symposium on Software Testing and Analysis (ISSTA)*. 67–77. DOI: 10.1145/2338965.2336762

Grosse, K., Papernot, N., Manoharan, P., Backes, M. and McDaniel, P. (2017) 'Adversarial examples for malware detection'. In *Proceedings of the European Symposium on Research in Computer Security. Lecture Notes in Computer Science*. 62–79. DOI: 10.1007/978-3-319-66399-9_4

Gruber, T. (1995) 'Towards principles for the design of ontologies used for knowledge sharing'. *International Journal of Human-Computer Studies*, 43 (5–6). 907–928.

Gruninger, M. and Fox, M. (1995) 'Methodologies for the design and evaluation of ontologies'. In *Proceedings of the International Joint Conference on Artificial Intelligence (IJCAI) Workshop*. 1–10.

Grzymek, V. and Puntschuh, M. (2019) 'What Europe knows and thinks about algorithms: Results of a representative survey'. Bertelsmann Stiftung. Available from: https://www.bertelsmann-stiftung.de/fileadmin/files/BSt/Publikationen/GrauePublikationen/WhatEuropeKnowsAndThinkAboutAlgorithm.pdf

*The Guardian* (2004) 'Why are men worse drivers than women?' Available from: https://www.theguardian.com/science/2004/may/13/thisweekssciencequestions1

Guizzardi, G. (2005) 'Ontological foundations for structural conceptual models'. Telematica Instituut Fundamental Research Series, No. 015 (TI/FRS/015). 1–416.

Hao, K. (2019) 'There's an easy way to make lending fairer for women. Trouble is, it's illegal'. Available from: https://www.technologyreview.com/2019/11/15/131935/theres-an-easy-way-to-make-lending-fairer-for-women-trouble-is-its-illegal/

Herbold, S. and Haar, T. (2022) 'Smoke testing for machine learning: Simple tests to discover severe defects'. *Empirical Software Engineering*, 27. 45. DOI: 10.1007/s10664-021-10073-7

High-Level Expert Group on Artificial Intelligence (2020) 'Ethics guidelines for trustworthy AI'. Available from: https://www.aepd.es/sites/default/files/2019-12/ai-ethics-guidelines.pdf

Hohenecker, P. and Lukasiewicz, T. (2020) 'Ontology reasoning with deep neural networks'. *Journal of Artificial Intelligence Research*, 68. 503–540.

Holzinger, A., Kieseberg, P., Weippl, E. and Tjoa, A. M. (2018) 'Current advances, trends and challenges of machine learning and knowledge extraction: From machine learning to explainable AI'. In *Proceedings of the International Cross-Domain Conference for Machine Learning and Knowledge Extraction*. 1–8.

Horridge, M. (2011) 'A practical guide to building OWL ontologies using Protégé 4 and CO-ODE tools'. 1.3 ed. Available from: http://owl.cs.manchester.ac.uk/research/co-ode/

Horridge, M. and Bechhofer, S. (2011) 'The OWL API: A Java API for OWL ontologies'. *Semantic Web*, 2 (1). 11–21.

Huh, M., Agrawal, P. and Efros, A. A. (2016) 'What makes ImageNet good for transfer learning?' Available from: http://arxiv.org/abs/1608.08614

Huo, Q., Zhu, H. and Greenwood, S. (2003) 'A multi-agent software engineering environment for testing web-based applications'. In *Proceedings of IEEE International Computer Software and Applications Conference*. 210–215.

IBM Cloud Education (2020) 'AIOps'. Available from: https://www.ibm.com/uk-en/cloud/learn/aiops

IEEE (2008) 'IEEE 829-2008 – IEEE Standard for software and system test documentation'. Available from: https://standards.ieee.org/standard/829-2008.html

IEEE (2015) 'IEEE 1872-2015 – IEEE Standard ontologies for robotics and automation'. Available from: https://standards.ieee.org/standard/1872-2015.html

IEEE (2020) 'IEEE 7010-2020 – IEEE Recommended practice for assessing the impact of autonomous and intelligent systems on human well-being'. Available from: https://standards.ieee.org/standard/7010-2020.html

Imana, B., Korolova, A. and Heidemann, J. (2021) 'Auditing for discrimination in algorithms delivering job ads'. In *Proceedings of the ACM Web Conference (WWW)*. 3767–3778. DOI: 10.1145/3442381.3450077

Institute and Faculty of Actuaries (2018) 'Continuous mortality investigation'. CMI 2017 Briefing note. Available from: https://www.actuaries.org.uk/learn-and-develop/continuous-mortality-investigation/cmiworking-papers/mortality-projections/cmi-working-paper-105

International Software Testing Qualifications Board (ISTQB) (2021). Available from: https://www.istqb.org

Ishikawa, F. and Yoshioka, N. (2019) 'How do engineers perceive difficulties in engineering of machine-learning systems? Questionnaire survey'. In *Proceedings of the IEEE/ACM Joint International Workshop on Conducting Empirical Studies in Industry (CESI) and the International Workshop on Software Engineering Research and Industrial Practice (SER&IP)*. 2–9. DOI: 10.1109/CESSER-IP.2019.00009

ISO (2005) 'ISO 9000:2005 Quality management systems – Fundamentals and vocabulary'. Available from: https://www.iso.org/obp/ui/#iso:std:iso:9000:ed-3:v1:en

ISO/IEC (2011) 'ISO/IEC 25010:2011 Systems and software engineering – Systems and software Quality Requirements and Evaluation (SQuaRE)'. Available from: https://www.iso.org/standard/35733.html

ISO/IEC (2017) 'ISO/IEC/IEEE 12207:2017 Systems and software engineering – Software life cycle processes'. Available from: https://www.iso.org/standard/63712.html

ISO/IEC (2020) 'ISO/IEC TR 29119-11:2020 Software and systems engineering – Software testing – Part 11: Guidelines on the testing of AI-based systems'. Available from: https://www.iso.org/standard/79016.html

ISO/IEC (2021a) 'ISO/IEC DIS 22989 – Information technology – Artificial intelligence – Artificial intelligence concepts and terminology'. Available from: https://www.iso.org/standard/74296.html

ISO/IEC (2021b) 'ISO/IEC TR 24027:2021 Information technology – Artificial intelligence (AI) – Bias in AI systems and AI aided decision making'. Available from: https://www.iso.org/standard/77607.html

ISO/IEC (2021c) 'ISO/IEC CD 25059: Software engineering – Systems and software Quality Requirements and Evaluation (SQuaRE) – Quality model for AI systems'. Available from: https://www.iso.org/cms/render/live/en/sites/isoorg/contents/data/standard/08/06/80655.html

ISO/IEC (2022) 'ISO/IEC DTR 24368 Information technology – Artificial intelligence – Overview of ethical and societal concerns'. Available from: https://www.iso.org/standard/78507.html

ISO/IEC/IEEE (2013a) 'ISO/IEC/IEEE 29119-1:2013 Software and systems engineering – Software testing – Part 1: Concepts and definitions'. Available from: https://www.iso.org/standard/45142.html

ISO/IEC/IEEE (2013b) 'ISO/IEC/IEEE 29119-2:2013 Software and systems engineering – Software testing – Part 2: Test processes'. Available from: https://www.iso.org/standard/56736.html

ISO/IEC/IEEE (2013c) 'ISO/IEC/IEEE 29119-3:2013 Software and systems engineering – Software testing – Part 3: Test documentation'. Available from: https://www.iso.org/standard/56737.html

ISO/IEC/IEEE (2015) 'ISO/IEC/IEEE 29119-4:2015 Software and systems engineering – Software testing – Part 4: Test techniques'. Available from: https://www.iso.org/standard/60245.html

ISO/IEC/IEEE (2017) 'ISO/IEC/IEEE 24765:2017 Systems and software engineering – Vocabulary'. Available from: https://www.iso.org/standard/71952.html

ISTQB (2021) 'Glossary'. Available from: https://glossary.istqb.org/en/search/

Jia, Y., Mao, K. and Harmon, M. (2018) 'Finding and fixing software bugs automatically with SapFix and Sapienz'. Available from: https://engineering.fb.com/2018/09/13/developer-tools/finding-and-fixing-software-bugs-automatically-with-sapfix-and-sapienz/

Juergens, E., Hummel, B., Deissenboeck, F., Feilkas, M., Schlögel, C. and Wübbeke, A. (2011) 'Regression test selection of manual system tests in practice'. In *Proceedings of the IEEE European Conference on Software Maintenance and Reengineering (CSMR)*. 309–312. DOI: 10.1109/CSMR.2011.44

Katsumi, M. and Gruninger, M. (2016) 'What is ontology reuse?' In *Proceedings of the International Conference on Formal Ontology in Information Systems (FOIS)*. 9–22.

Khan, J. H., Magnetti, S., Davis, E. and Zhang, J. (2000) 'Late outcomes of open heart surgery in patients 70 years old or later'. *The Annals of Thoracic Surgery*, 69 (1). 165–170. Available from: https://www.annalsthoracicsurgery.org/article/S0003-4975(99)01185-6/fulltext#relatedArticles

Kinsbruner, E. (2020) *Accelerating Software Quality: Machine Learning and Artificial Intelligence in the Age of DevOps.* Perforce.

Kloumann, I. and Tanner, J. (2021) 'How we're using Fairness Flow to help build AI that works better for everyone'. Facebook AI. Available from: https://ai.facebook.com/blog/how-were-using-fairness-flow-to-help-build-ai-that-works-better-for-everyone/

Klueck, F., Li, Y., Nica, M., Tao, J. and Wotawa, F. (2018) 'Using ontologies for test suites generation for automated and autonomous driving functions'. In *Proceedings of the IEEE International Symposium on Software Reliability Engineering Workshops*. 1–6.

Koch, C. (2016) 'How the computer beat the Go Master'. *Scientific American.* Available from: https://www.scientificamerican.com/article/how-the-computer-beat-the-go-master/

Kogut, P., Cranefield, S., Hart, L., Dutra, M., Baclawski, K., Kokar, M. and Smith, J. (2002) 'UML for ontology development'. *The Knowledge Engineering Review*, 17 (1). 61–64.

Koh, L., Orzes, G. and Jia, F. J. (2019) 'The fourth industrial revolution (Industry 4.0): Technologies disruption on operations and supply chain management'. *International Journal of Operations and Production Management*, 39 (6–8). 817–828.

Krisher (2019) 'Official: Safety lacking before Uber self-driving car crash'. *Techxplore.* Available from: https://techxplore.com/news/2019-11-safety-lacking-uber-self-driving-car.html

Kuleshov, A. (2018) 'Formalizing AI system parameters in standardization of AI'. In *Proceedings of the IEEE International Conference on Artificial Intelligence Applications and Innovations (IC-AIAI)*. 51–54.

Kurakin, A., Goodfellow, I. and Bengio, S. (2017) 'Adversarial machine learning at scale'. Available from: http://arxiv.org/abs/1611.01236

Kuwajima, H. and Ishikawa, F. (2019) 'Adapting SQuaRE for quality assessment of artificial intelligence systems'. In *Proceedings of the IEEE International Symposium on Software Reliability Engineering Workshops (ISSREW)*. 13–18. DOI: 10.1109/ISSREW.2019.00035

Landhausser, M. and Genaid, A. (2012) 'Connecting user stories and code for test development'. In *Proceedings of the IEEE International Workshop on Recommendation Systems for Software Engineering*. 33–37.

Larson, J., Mattu, S., Kirchner, L. and Angwin, J. (2016) 'How we analyzed the COMPAS recidivism algorithm'. *ProPublica.* Available from: https://www.propublica.org/article/how-we-analyzed-the-compas-recidivism-algorithm

Lenarduzzi, V., Lomio, F., Moreschini, S., Taibi, D. and Tamburri, D. A. (2021). 'Software quality for AI: Where we are now?' In D. Winkler, S. Biffl, D. Mendez, M. Wimmer and J. Bergsmann (eds). *Software Quality: Future Perspectives on Software Engineering Quality*, vol. 404. Springer International Publishing. 43–53. DOI: 10.1007/978-3-030-65854-0_4

Li, H., Chen, F., Yang, H., Guo, H., Chu, W. C.-C. and Yang, Y. (2009) 'An ontology-based approach for GUI testing'. In *Proceedings of the IEEE International Computer Software and Applications Conference*. 632–633.

Lim, X. and Zhang, W. (2012) 'Ontology-based testing platform for reusing'. In *Proceedings of the IEEE International Conference on Internet Computing for Science and Engineering*. 86–89.

Linux Test Project (LTP) (2021). Available from: https://github.com/linux-test-project/ltp

Looker, N., Gwynne, B., Xu, J. and Munro, M. (2005) 'An ontology-based approach for determining the dependability of service-oriented architectures'. In *Proceedings of the Annual IEEE International Workshop on Object-Oriented Real-Time Dependable Systems*. 1–8.

Lu, D. (2020) 'Uber and Lyft pricing algorithms charge more in non-white areas'. *New Scientist.* Available from: https://www.newscientist.com/article/2246202-uber-and-lyft-pricing-algorithms-charge-more-in-non-white-areas/

Ma, M., Wang, P. and Chu, C.-H. (2014) 'Ontology-based semantic modeling and evaluation for Internet of Things applications'. In *Proceedings of the IEEE International Conference on Green Computing and Communications*. 24–30.

Maedche, A. and Staab, S. (2004) 'Ontology learning'. In *Handbook on Ontologies*. Springer. 173–190.

Manifesto for Software Craftsmanship (n.d.). Available from: https://manifesto.softwarecraftsmanship.org

Martin, R. C. (2008) *Clean Code: A Handbook of Agile Software Craftsmanship*. Prentice Hall.

McDonald, S. (2015) 'Indirect gender discrimination and the "Test-Achats Ruling": An Examination of the UK motor insurance market'. Presentation to the Royal Economic Society. Available from: https://editorialexpress.com/cgi-bin/conference/download.cgi?db_name=RES2015&paper_id=791

Merriam-Webster (2021) 'Non-fungible token'. Available from: https://www.merriam-webster.com/dictionary/non-fungible%20token

Metz, C. (2019) 'We teach A.I. systems everything, including our biases'. *New York Times*. Available from: https://www.nytimes.com/2019/11/11/technology/artificial-intelligence-bias.html

MMC (2019) 'The State of AI: Divergence'. Available from: https://www.stateofai2019.com/

Murtazinam, M. S. and Avdeenko, T. V. (2018) 'The ontology-driven approach to support the requirements engineering process in Scrum framework'. *CEUR-WS 2212*. 287–295.

Nasser, V. H., Du, W. and MacIsaac, D. (2010) 'An ontology-based software test generation framework'. In *Proceedings of the IEEE International Conference on Software Engineering and Knowledge Engineering (SEKE)*. 192–197.

Newberry, C. (2019) 'The Facebook Pixel: What it is and how to use it'. Available from: https://blog.hootsuite.com/facebook-pixel/

Nie, C. and Leung, H. (2011) 'A survey of combinatorial testing'. *ACM Computing Surveys*, 43 (2). 1–29. DOI: 10.1145/1883612.1883618

Nor, M. Z. M., Abdullah, R., Selamat, M. H. and Murad, M. A. A. (2012) 'An agent-based knowledge management system for collaborative software maintenance environment design and evaluation'. In *Proceedings of the IEEE International Conference on Information Retrieval and Knowledge Management*. 115–120.

Northcutt, C. G., Athalye, A. and Mueller, J. (2021) 'Pervasive label errors in test sets destabilize machine learning benchmarks'. In *Proceedings of the Neural Information Processing Systems Track on Datasets and Benchmarks 1 Pre-Proceedings (NeurIPS Datasets and Benchmarks)*. 1–13.

Noy, N. and McGuinness, L. (2001) 'Ontology development 101: A guide to creating your first ontology'. Available from: http://protege.stanford.edu/publications/ontology_development/ontology101.pdf

Olivares-Alarcos, A., Bessler, D., Khamis, A., Goncalves, P., Habib, M., Bermejo-Alonso, J., Barreto, M., Diab, M., Rosell, J., Quintas, J., Olszewska, J. I., Nakawala, H., Pignaton de Freitas, E., Gyrard, A., Borgo, S., Alenya, G., Beetz, M. and Li, H. (2019) 'A review and comparison of ontology-based approaches to robot autonomy'. *The Knowledge Engineering Review*, 34. 1–38.

Olszewska, J. I. (2011) 'Spatio-temporal visual ontology'. In *EPSRC/BMVA Workshop on Vision and Language (VL)*. 1–2.

Olszewska, J. I. (2015) 'UML activity diagrams for OWL ontology building'. In *Proceedings of the International Conference on Knowledge Engineering and Ontology Development, 2*. 370–374.

Olszewska, J. I. (2018a) 'Ontologies for vision agents'. In *IEEE International Conference on Intelligent Robots and Systems (IROS)*.

Olszewska, J. I. (2018b) 'Ontologies for intelligent vision systems'. In *International Conference on Knowledge Engineering and Ontology Development (KEOD)*. Available from: http://www.keod.ic3k.org/Tutorials.aspx?y=2018

Olszewska, J. I. (2018c) 'Visual ontologies for intelligent robotics'. In *BMVA Symposium on Enabling Human-Level Understanding in Robots*.

Olszewska, J. I. (2019a) 'Designing transparent and autonomous intelligent vision systems'. In *Proceedings of the International Conference on Agents and Artificial Intelligence*. 850–856.

Olszewska, J. I. (2019b) 'D7-R4: Software development life-cycle for intelligent vision systems'. In *Proceedings of the International Conference on Knowledge Engineering and Ontology Development*. 435–441.

Olszewska, J. I. (2020) 'AI-T: Software testing ontology for AI-based systems'. In *Proceedings of the International Conference on Knowledge Engineering and Ontology Development*. 291–298.

Olszewska, J. I. and Allison, I. K. (2018). 'ODYSSEY: Software development lifecycle ontology'. In *Proceedings of the International Conference on Knowledge Engineering and Ontology Development*. 303–311.

Olszewska, J. I. and McCluskey, T. L. (2011) 'Ontology-coupled active contours for dynamic video scene understanding'. In *Proceedings of the IEEE International Conference on Intelligent Engineering Systems*. 369–374.

Olszewska, J. I., Houghtaling, M., Goncalves, P., Fabiano, N., Haidegger, T., Carbonera, J. L., Patterson, W. R., Ragavan, S. V., Fiorini, S. and Prestes, E. (2020) 'Robotic standard development life cycle in action'. *Journal of Intelligent & Robotic Systems, 98* (1). 119–131.

Olszewska, J. I., Houghtaling, M., Goncalves, P., Haidegger, T., Fabiano, N., Carbonera, J. L., Fiorini, S. and Prestes, E. (2018) 'Robotic ontological standard development life cycle'. In *IEEE International Conference on Robotics and Automation (ICRA)*. 1–6.

Olszewska, J. I., Simpson, R. M. and McCluskey, T. L. (2014) 'Dynamic OWL ontology design based on UML and BPMN'. In *Proceedings of the International Conference on Knowledge Engineering and Ontology Development*. 436–444.

Pandey, A. and Caliskan, A. (2020) 'Iterative effect-size bias in ridehailing: Measuring social bias in dynamic pricing of 100 million rides'. Available from: https://arxiv.org/abs/2006.04599

Pandey, C. and Caliskan, A. (2021) 'Disparate impact of artificial intelligence bias in ridehailing economy's price discrimination algorithms'. In *Proceedings of the AAAI/ACM Conference on Artificial Intelligence, Ethics, and Society*. 822–833.

PathCheck Foundation (n.d.). Available from: https://www.pathcheck.org/

Paydar, S. and Kahani, M. (2010) 'Ontology-based web application testing'. In *Proceedings of IEEE Conference on Novel Algorithms and Techniques in Telecommunications and Networking.* 23–27.

Perry, T. (2019) 'San Diego's connected street lights learn to spot bicycles'. Available from: https://spectrum.ieee.org/view-from-the-valley/computing/software/san-diegos-streetlights-are-now-counting-bicycles

Petrucci, G., Ghidini, C. and Rospocher, M. (2016) 'Ontology learning in the deep'. In *Proceedings of the European Knowledge Acquisition Workshop.* 480–495.

Pignaton de Freitas, E., Bermejo-Alonso, J., Khamis, A., Li, H. and Olszewska, J. I. (2020a) 'Ontologies for cloud robotics'. *The Knowledge Engineering Review,* 35. 1–19.

Pignaton de Freitas, E., Olszewska, J. I., Carbonera, J., Fiorini, S. R., Khamis, A., Ragavan, S. V., Barreto, M., Prestes, E., Habib, M. K., Redfield, S., Chibani, A., Goncalves, P., Bermejo-Alonso, J., Sanz, R., Tosello, E., Olivares-Alarcos, A., Konzen, A. A., Quintas, J. and Li, H. (2020b) 'Ontological concepts for information sharing in cloud robotics'. *Journal of Ambient Intelligence and Humanized Computing.* 1–14. DOI: 10.1007/s12652-020-02150-4

Pinto, H. S. (1999) 'Towards ontology reuse'. In *Proceedings of AAAI Workshop on Ontology Management.* 67–73.

PK, M. A., Sheriff, M. R. and Chatterjee, D. (2021) 'Measure of quality of finite-dimensional linear systems: A frame-theoretic view'. *Systems & Control Letters,* 151. 104911. DOI: 10.1016/j.sysconle.2021.104911

Pop, C., Moldovan, D., Antal, M., Valea, D., Cioara, T., Anghel, I. and Salomie, I. (2014) 'M2O: A library for using ontologies in software engineering'. In *Proceedings of the IEEE International Conference on Intelligent Computer Communication and Processing.* 69–75.

Portoraro, F. (2021) 'Automated reasoning'. In *The Stanford Encyclopedia of Philosophy* (Fall 2021 edition). Edward N. Zalta (ed.). Available from: https://plato.stanford.edu/archives/fall2021/entries/reasoning-automated/

Principles of Chaos Engineering (2019). Available from: https://principlesofchaos.org/

Protégé tool website (2021). Available from: http://protege.stanford.edu/

Resource Description Framework (RDF) (2021). Available from: https://www.w3.org/RDF/

Ritchson, M. (2021) 'Teamwork, AI, and containerization (with NASA's Michael Ritchson)'. The QA Lead Podcast. Available from: TheQALead.com/Podcasts

Robal, T., Marenkov, J. and Kalja, A. (2017) 'Ontology design for automatic evaluation of web user interface usability'. In *Proceedings of the IEEE Portland International Conference on Management of Engineering and Technology.* 1–8.

Rocha Silva, T., Hak, J.-L. and Winckler, M. (2017) 'A behavior-based ontology for supporting automated assessment of interactive systems'. In *Proceedings of the IEEE International Conference on Semantic Computing.* 250–257.

Rothstein, R. (2017) *The Color of Law.* Liveright.

Sampath Kumar, V. R., Khamis, A., Fiorini, S. R., Carbonera, J. L., Olivares-Alarcos, A., Habib, M., Goncalves, P., Li, H. and Olszewska, J. I. (2019) 'Ontologies for Industry 4.0'. *The Knowledge Engineering Review*, 34. 1–14.

Sapna, P. G. and Mohanty, H. (2011) 'An ontology based approach for test scenario management'. In *Proceedings of the International Conference on Information Intelligence, Systems, Technology and Management*. 91–100.

Seeliger, A., Pfaff, M. and Krcmar, H. (2019) 'Semantic web technologies for explainable machine learning models: A literature review'. In *International Semantic Web Conference (ISWC)*. 30–45.

Serrano, J. (2022) 'Airbnb will hide guests' first names in Oregon until bookings are confirmed to fight discrimination'. Available from: https://gizmodo.com/airbnb-will-hide-guests-first-names-in-oregon-until-bo-1848294121

Shankar, S., Halpern, Y., Breck, E., Atwood, J., Wilson, J. and Sculley, D. (2017) 'No classification without representation: Assessing geodiversity issues in open data sets for the developing world'. Available from: https://arxiv.org/abs/1711.08536

Šidak, Z. (1968) 'On multivariate normal probabilities of rectangles: Their dependence on correlations'. *Annals of Mathematical Statistics*, 39. 1425–1434.

Simmons, C. B., Shiva, S. G. and Simmons, L. L. (2014) 'A qualitative analysis of an ontology based issue resolution system for cyber attack management'. In *Proceedings of the IEEE International Conference on Cyber Technology in Automation, Control and Intelligent*. 323–329.

Simpson, E. H. (1951) 'The interpretation of interaction in contingency tables'. *Journal of the Royal Statistical Society. Series B (Methodological)*, 13 (2). 238–241.

Siqueira Bueno, P. M., de Franco Rosa, F., Jino, M. and Bonacin, R. (2018) 'A security testing process supported by an ontology environment: A conceptual proposal'. In *Proceedings of the IEEE/ACS International Conference on Computer Systems and Applications*. 1–8.

Slee, D., Cain, S., Vichare, P. and Olszewska, J. I. (2021) 'Smart lifts: An ontological approach'. In *Proceedings of the International Conference on Knowledge Engineering and Ontology Development*. 210–219.

Smith, A. (2018) 'Public attitudes toward computer algorithms'. Pew Research Center. Available from: https://www.pewresearch.org/internet/2018/11/16/public-attitudes-toward-computer-algorithms/

Spocchia, G. and Morris, H. (2020) 'Revealed: The "daylight robbery"of school holiday price increases'. *The Telegraph*. Available from: https://www.telegraph.co.uk/travel/news/half-term-holiday-prices/

Staab, S. and Maedche, A. (2000) 'Ontology engineering beyond the modeling of concepts and relations'. In *Proceedings of the European Conference on Artificial Intelligence (ECAI) Workshop*. 1–6.

Steed, R. and Caliskan, A. (2021) 'Image representations learned with unsupervised pre-training contain human-like biases'. In *ACM Conference on Fairness Accountability and Transparency (FAccT '21)*. 701–713. DOI: 10.1145/3442188.3445932

Stokel-Walker, C. (2021) 'Recruiters less likely to contact ethnic minority groups on Swiss site'. *New Scientist.* Available from: https://www.newscientist.com/article/2265372-recruiters-less-likely-to-contact-ethnic-minority-groups-on-swiss-site/

Sugawara, K., Manabe, Y., Moulin, C. and Barthes, J.-P. (2011) 'Design assistant agents for supporting requirement specification definition in a distributed design team'. In *Proceedings of the IEEE International Conference on Computer Supported Cooperative Work in Design*. 329–334.

Suggested Upper Merged Ontology (SUMO) (2021). Available from: www.ontologyportal.org/

Thrun, S. (2018) 'Reputation in the age of artificial intelligence'. PRSA. Available from: https://apps.prsa.org/StrategiesTactics/Articles/view/12194/1155/Reputation_in_the_Age_of_Artificial_Intelligence#.YajjKJH7S2I

Tiffany, R. (2020) 'Fighting COVID-19 with digital twins'. YouTube, 9 April 2020. Available from: https://youtu.be/XKINvqiTgxQ

Tsarkov, D. (2014) 'Incremental and persistent reasoning in FaCT++'. In *Proceedings of OWL Reasoner Evaluation Workshop*. 16–22.

Tudorache, T. (2020) 'Ontology engineering: Current state, challenges, and future directions'. *Semantic Web*, 11 (1). 125–138.

Uschold, M. and Gruninger, M. (1996) 'Ontologies: Principles, methods and applications'. *Knowledge Engineering Review*, 11 (2). 93–136.

Uschold, M., Healy, M., Williamson, K., Clark, P. and Woods, S. (1998) 'Ontology reuse and application'. In *Proceedings of the International Conference on Formal Ontology in Information Systems (FOIS)*. 179–192.

Vasilecas, O., Kalibatiene, D. and Guizzardi, G. (2009) 'Towards a formal method for the transformation of ontology axioms to application domain rules'. *Information Technology and Control*, 38 (4). 271–282.

Venkatadri, G., Andreou, A., Liu, Y., Mislove, A., Gummadi, K., Loiseau, P. and Goga, O. (2018) 'Privacy risks with Facebook's PII-based targeting: Auditing a data broker's advertising interface'. In *Proceedings of the IEEE Symposium on Security and Privacy*. 89–107.

Vincent, J. (2016) 'Twitter taught Microsoft's AI chatbot to be a racist asshole in less than a day'. *The Verge.* Available from: https://www.theverge.com/2016/3/24/11297050/tay-microsoft-chatbot-racist

Wang, X., Huang, N. and Wang, R. (2009) 'Mutation test based on OWL-S requirement model'. In *Proceedings of the IEEE International Conference on Web Services*. 1006–1007.

Wang, Y., Bai, X., Li, J. and Huang, R. (2007) 'Ontology-based test case generation for testing web services'. In *Proceedings of the IEEE International Symposium on Autonomous Decentralized Systems*. 43–50.

Ward, E. J. (2020) 'Abandoned NHS contact tracing app cost almost £12 million'. LBC. Available from: https://www.lbc.co.uk/politics/abandoned-nhs-contact-tracing-app-cost-almost-12-million/

Web Ontology Language (OWL) (2021). Available from: https://www.w3.org/OWL/

Wikipedia (2020) 'Trolley problem'. Available from: https://en.wikipedia.org/w/index.php?title=Trolley_problem&oldid=987726957

Wikipedia (2021) 'All-pairs testing'. Available from: https://en.wikipedia.org/wiki/All-pairs_testing

Wilson, K. M., Helton, W. S. and Wiggins, M. W. (2013) 'Cognitive engineering'. *Wiley Interdisciplinary Reviews: Cognitive Science*, 4 (1). 17–31.

Winfield, A. F. T., Booth, S., Dennis, L. A., Egawa, T., Hastie, H., Jacobs, N., Muttram, R., Olszewska, J. I., Rajabiyazdi, F., Theodorou, A., Underwood, M., Wortham, R. H. and Watson, E. (2021) 'IEEE P7001: A proposed standard on transparency'. *Frontiers on Robotics and AI*, 8. 1–16.

Wisniewski, D., Potoniec, J., Lawrynowicz, A. and Keet, C. M. (2019) 'Analysis of ontology competency questions and their formalizations in SPARQL-OWL'. *Journal of Web Semantics*, 59. 1–19.

Wos, L., Overbeck, R., Lusk, E. and Boyle, J. (2021) 'Automated reasoning: Introduction and applications'. U.S. Department of Energy – Office of Scientific and Technical Information. Available from: https://www.osti.gov/biblio/6003867

Wright, J. (2016a) 'STARWest - Think you can just "Test" that API? Think again'. YouTube. Available from: https://youtu.be/Xu-rXUJ4IOQ

Wright, J. (2016b) 'The Digital Manifesto'. Available from: https://leanpub.com/digital

Wright, J. (2017) 'Cognitive Learning – "Digital Evolution, Over Revolution"'. TEDxWilmingtonSalon. Available from: https://www.ted.com/talks/jonathon_wright_cognitive_learning_digital_evolution_over_revolution

Wu, D. and Hakansson, A. (2014) 'A method of identifying ontology domain'. *Procedia Computer Science*, 35. 504–513.

Yan, H., Jing, Z., Li-Qun, Y., Ze-Min, L. and Li-Jian, T. (2014) 'Based on ontology methodology to model and evaluate System of Systems (SoS)'. In *Proceedings of the IEEE International Conference on System of Systems Engineering (SOSE)*. 101–106.

Yu, L., Zhang, L., Xiang, H., Su, Y., Zhao, W. and Zhu, J. (2009) 'A framework of testing as a service'. In *Proceedings of the IEEE International Conference on Management and Service Science*. 1–4.

Zimmermann, T., Nagappan, N., Gall, H., Giger, E. and Murphy, B. (2009) 'Cross-project defect prediction: A large scale experiment on data vs. domain vs. process'. In *Proceedings of the ACM Joint Meeting of the European Software Engineering Conference and the ACM SIGSOFT Symposium on the Foundations of Software Engineering*. 91–100. DOI: 10.1145/1595696.1595713

Zuckerberg, M. (2021) 'Introducing Meta: A social technology company'. Available from: https://about.fb.com/news/2021/10/facebook-company-is-now-meta

# INDEX

Page numbers in italics refer to figures and tables.